英语写作常识与实践

李安勤　主编

武汉理工大学出版社

·武　汉·

内 容 提 要

本书内容分为两编。第一编为英语语言文字与写作的常识性知识，包括标点符号的正确使用和移行规则、段落的基本知识与写作技巧、英语句子的常见错误及修改方法和英语文章提纲的撰写。第二编的主要内容为英语写作的四大文体：记叙文、议论文、描写文和说明文。这一部分主要介绍英语的四大文体和写作方法。本书是一本具有工具书性质的教科书。

图书在版编目(CIP)数据

英语写作常识与实践 / 李安勤主编. — 武汉 : 武汉理工大学出版社, 2023.11
ISBN 978-7-5629-6932-7

Ⅰ.①英… Ⅱ.①李… Ⅲ.①英语－写作 Ⅳ.①H315

中国国家版本馆CIP数据核字（2023）第236095号

项目负责人：王兆国　　　　责任编辑：史卫国
责任校对：雷红娟　　　　　排　版：米　乐
出版发行：武汉理工大学出版社
社　　址：武汉市洪山区珞狮路122号
邮　　编：430070
网　　址：http：//www.wutp.com.cn
经　　销：各地新华书店
印　　刷：北京亚吉飞数码科技有限公司
开　　本：170×240　1/16
印　　张：12.75
字　　数：202千字
版　　次：2024年6月第1版
印　　次：2024年6月第1次印刷
定　　价：82.00元

前　言

　　笔者长期从事英语写作教学，对于英语写作学习中的痛点和难点与英语写作初学者感同身受。一方面是写作初学者的词汇量与表达法储备不足，另一方面是读本中的范文难度太大，不符合初学者的实际能力，写作初学者在学习写作技能的同时还要花大量时间消化书中的生词，大大降低了学习效率。基于此，本书专门采用中文编写，循序渐进地安排学习难度，尊重学习规律。为了保护、培养学生的学习兴趣，本书在段落学习阶段大大降低范文的难度，教会初学者写身边的事、当下的事；同时，书中融入了文化自信、爱国主义和传统传承的教育内容，如小学语文课文《参观人民大会堂》和中学语文课文中的清代小说《狼》。

　　英语书面语学习根据其能力目标可以分解为阅读能力、书面语基础知识和英语的写作能力等几个方面。英语写作可分为两大块，即写作基础知识（basic knowledge of writing）和格式文体写作（essay writing）。写作基础知识包含文字书写与基本写作技能，涉及书写规范、语法、语用、修辞和书面语书写规范等内容。本书将段落和文章提纲的构思及创作方法也纳入写作基础知识的范畴。

　　格式文体写作（essay writing）又叫高级写作，一般认为它指的是英语中的记叙文、描写文、议论文和说明文四大文体写作。高级写作是建立在掌握英语写作基础技能基础上的写作能力的综合运用，就是我们所说的"做文章"，它与写作基础知识与基本技能有着本质的区别。做文章是一种需要较高技巧和能力的高级脑力活动。

　　本书将遣词与造句部分放在"英语句子常见语病及修改"一章中。标点

1

符号是语言文字的重要组成部分，英语写作中难免需要移行，然而长期以来标点符号的使用与移行规则在我国的英语教学中是一个"真空地带"。为了改变这种状况，本书中将标点符号的正确使用和英语的移行规则纳入正规写作学习中。

本书还对写作理论与实践中一些长期模糊的名词与概念进行了厘清与规范。如controlling idea中文定名为"规定性信息"、order of sentences 定名为"条理性"、order of importance 定名为"主次顺序"、fused sentence 定名为"无标点句"、comma splice定名为"万能逗号句"。run-on sentence 这个概念我国学术界长期认为指fused sentence和comma splice，实际上它只能指fused sentence。在四大文体的英语名称中，不提倡使用narration，argumentation，description和exposition。讲英语国家语文学科中有它们专有的说法叫narrative，argumentative，descriptive 和expository。

本书适用于高职高专、大学低年级英语写作的学习、阅读，以及高中英语的书面表达学习，大学四六级写作考试的学子和其他学习者也可以参阅。

本人才疏学浅，不揣浅陋，书中疏漏与不足之处在所难免，恳请广大同仁、读者批评斧正。本书中引用或参考的书目均已在参考文献中列出并在此深深致谢。除少数习题题型外所有涉及他人的资料均已注明出处。

作者

2023年8月

目 录

第一编　英语写作常识

第二编　英语文体写作

第一编
英语写作常识

第一章　英语的段落

段落（paragraph）是构成文章的基本单位。段落写得好不好，直接关系到文章的质量高低。段落的写作应该做到结构合理、思路清晰，句子的表述应符合逻辑且安排有序、突出主题、没有语病。掌握娴熟的写作技巧在英语写作中尤其重要。

在段落写作学习中，应遵循以下原则，即**用简单的词汇、简单的句型写出简单的段落，表达出清楚的意思**。段落写作要使用"拿得准"的单词和句子，清楚地表达简单的思想，不追求华丽的辞藻。所谓"拿得准"，就是指明白单词的意思，掌握一个单词或短语的内涵外延，同时对它的用法十分了解，保证在一定的语境中不会用词不当或词不达意。句子结构也是如此，要使用常见的、正确的句型，不要发明句型，造成错误，令读者不明所云。语言的本质就是一个群体所有成员共同接受并通用的一套语音符号系统和记录口头语言的书面符号系统，具有较强的社会属性，语言表达要通俗易懂。

英语中的段落通常由主题句、支撑句和结尾句组成。主题句提出本段论述的主题，是核心句，支撑句围绕主题句提供细节性的描述，对主题句加以说明和论证，最后在结尾句中根据支撑句的论证得出结论，与主题句遥相呼应，构成一个完整的段落。

第一节　主题句

主题句（topic sentence）是点明主题、为全段立意的句子，是整个段落的灵魂。它具有概括性、提示性、规定性和完整性。主题句凝练了一段的主题思想，提示读者这一段要说什么，同时主题句还有一定的规定性，它规定该段的写作要围绕主题句展开，要服务于主题，通过对主题的支撑、说明、演绎和拓展，完整地表达出本段的主题。

主题句本身必须具有完整性，能完整、明白无误地表达一个主题，也就是全段的中心思想。由于要高度概括，它不能描写细节，但是也不能太笼统、范围太广，失去了对支撑句的规定作用。

主题句是全段纲领性的句子。通常出现在段落的第一句，但少数情况下也可以出现在段落中间或最后。例如：

I had a busy day yesterday.

本句中，I点明主题（topic）"我"，had a busy day yesterday是本句的规定性信息（controlling idea），为本句定下了基本格调，规定本段写昨天忙了些什么、是怎么忙的。

My mother is a warm-hearted woman.

本句中，my mother是主题，a warm-hearted woman是规定性信息，所以本段后面的内容只能写我妈妈是怎么热情待人、乐于助人的，而不能写我妈妈如何关心我的生活、学习，或者我妈妈如何美丽大方。

假如你的文章题目是"我的妈妈"，全文就要全面地描述一下自己的妈妈美丽、勤劳、热情、热爱生活、关心家人，可以一段一段地来，每一段写一个方面。段落的主题句是某一段的主题，不是全文的主题。

【范文一】

I had a busy day yesterday. Before I went to bed the night before, I set the alarm clock to wake me up at six the next morning. After a brief breakfast, I went out to meet my classmates at the gate of the college. We were to go to a nearby primary school to teach the kids to sing English songs. I was in charge of ten of the pupils who were going to take part in the Kid's English Speaking Contest of the year, of which talent show was one part. Before beginning to sing, I told them to read the words while I corrected some of the mistakes in their pronunciation. To my surprise, I was told to teach the kids to dance, too. This was a tough task because I never learned dancing. I made some movements imitating the dancers I watched in TV programs and told the kids to follow me. At the end of the morning, I found they were doing pretty well. Their teachers said they looked forward to our coming again before saying goodbye. **We were tired but happy.**

【点评】

I had a busy day yesterday为本段的主题句，We were tired but happy为结尾句，其余句子为支撑句，用以说明、支撑主题。

【范文二】

My mother is a warm-hearted woman. She is always ready to help others and is very active in the affairs of our community. She often works as a matchmaker for young single neighbors and many married couples live happily together ever since blind dates arranged by her. Last summer, when an international game was held in our city she entered for the volunteer service and encouraged Dad and me to join in, too. We did a good job in helping those who came to the event. She was awarded the title of Outstanding Citizen by the municipal government last month. **She deserves it.**

【点评】

My mother is a warm-hearted woman为本段的主题句，She deserves it为结尾句，其余句子为支撑句。结尾句She deserces it较好地呼应了主题句。

【范文三】

English is very popular around the world. It is one of the work languages in the United Nations and is widely used in business situations as well as diplomatic ones. English is spoken by pilots and airport control operators on all the airways of the world. Over 70 percent of the world's mail is written in English. More than 60 percent of the world's radio programs are in English. **Clearly English is an international language.**

【点评】

English is very popular around the world为本段的主题句，Clearly English is an international language为结尾句响应主题句，其余句子为支撑句，用以支撑主题。

【范文四】

The institution of the foreign migrant worker appears around the

world when a relatively rich country is near a relatively poor one and there is access between them. Mexican farm workers in the United States, Algerian farm workers in France, Turkish laborers in Germany, and Ethiopian domestic servants in Kuwait are all examples. Each example shows the combined effects of overpopulation and unequal distribution of employment opportunity and wealth. In all cases, there are dangers that migrant workers will be exploited by local employers who recognize their vulnerability and that they will be resented by local workers who see them as competitors. Cesar Chavez organized the United Farm Workers union in California in response to such problems in 1962 and after a multiyear strike was able to obtain better wages and working conditions for grape pickers. **Similar unions have developed in many places around the world.**

【点评】

The institution of the foreign migrant worker appears around the world when a relatively rich country is near a relatively poor one and there is access between them为本段的主题句，其余为支撑句。主题句中的institution是工人联合会性质的组织，不是指政府的劳工管理部门，最后一句Similar unions have developed in many places around the world是结尾句，是对主题句很好的呼应。

阅读与练习

一、请找出下列段落中的主题句。

1. Smoking is harmful to your health. Experiments show that smoking can cause cancer. Besides the most serious disease cancer, smoking can also cause other health problems. For example, it gives one a "smoker's cough". Finally, studies have shown it is easy for smokers to catch colds. Whether you get an unimportant cold or the terrible killer, caner, smoking is harmful. It is worth it?

2. Albert Einstein, one of the world's greatest scientists, failed in his university entrance exam on his first attempt. William Faulkner, one of America's famous writers, never finished college because he could not pass his English

courses. Sir Winston Churchill, who is considered one of the masters of the English language, was very poor in English during middle school. These few examples show that school does not always predict failure in life.

3. In the past few years, social networking sites such as MySpace, Facebook, and Twitter have become hugely popular across all ages. Despite the opinions of some that young people are in danger of turning into crouching androids glued to their computers, research shows that the majority of friendships are still maintained offline. Offline friendships are characterized by more interdependence, depth, understanding, and commitment, but online friendships can gain some of these qualities with time. Most online friends tend to be rather cautious about disclosing personal information. However, this does not apply to people with a negative view of themselves and others; they instead seem to share more information, possibly in an attempt to become more self-confident in their interactions. Interestingly, even in online friendships people seem to gain more satisfaction when befriending people of a similar age and place of residence.

4. Drama languished in Europe after the fall of Rome during the fifth and sixth centuries. From about A.D. 400 to 900 almost no record of dramatic productions exists except for those of minstrels and other entertainers, such as acrobats and jugglers, who traveled through the countryside. The Catholic church was instrumental in suppressing drama because the theater—represented by the excesses of Roman productions—was seen as subversive. No state-sponsored festivals brought people together in huge theaters the way they had in Greek and Roman times.

5. One form of distraction is imagery. Creating a vivid mental image can help control pain or other unpleasant physical symptoms. Usually people create a pleasant and progressive scenario, such as walking along the beach, hiking in the mountains, or enjoying a gathering of friends. Aggressive or arousing imagery can also be useful, such as imagining a heated argument, fighting off an enemy, or driving a race car at high speeds. Whatever imaginary scenario you use, try to visualize all the different sensations involved, including the sights, sounds,

aromas, touches, and tastes. The goal is to become so absorbed in your fantasy that you distract yourself from the pain sensations.

I often dreamed about Pisa when I was a boy. I read about the famous building called the Leaning Tower of Pisa. But when I read the word Pisa, I was thinking of pizza. I thought this tower was a place to buy pizza. It must be the best place to buy pizza in the world, I thought.

Many years later I finally saw the Leaning Tower. I knew then that is was Pisa and not pizza. But there was still something special about it for me. The tower got its name because it really does lean to one side. Some people want to try to fix it. They are afraid it may fall over and they don't like it leans over the city.

I do not think it's a good idea to try to fix it. The tower probably will not fall down, it is 600 years old. Why should anything happen to it now? And, if you ask me, I like what it looks like. To me it is a very human kind of leaning. Nothing is perfect, it seems to say.

And who cares? Why do people want things to be perfect? Imperfect things may be more interesting. Let's take the tower in Pisa. Why is it so famous? There are many other older, more beautiful towers in Italy. But Pisa tower is the most famous. People come from all over the world to see it.

6. Surtsey was born in 1963. Scientists saw the birth of this island. It began at 7:30 a.m. on 14th November. A fishing boat was near Iceland. The boat moved under the captain's feet. He noticed a strange smell. He saw some black smoke. A volcano was breaking out. Red-hot rocks, fire and smoke were rushing up from the bottom of the sea. The island grew quickly. It was 10 meters high the next day and 60 meters high on 18th November. Scientists flew there to watch. It was exciting. Smoke and fire were still rushing up. Pieces of red-hot rock were flying into the air and falling into the sea. The sea was boiling and there was a strange light in the sky. Surtsey grew and grew. Then it stopped in June 1967. It was 175 meters high and 2 kilometers long. And life was already coming to Surtsey. Plants grew. Birds came. Some scientists built a house. They want to learn about this young island. A new island is like a new world.

7. We can make mistakes at any age. Some mistakes we make are about money, but most mistakes are about people. "Did Jerry really care when I broke up with Helen?" "When I got that great job, did Jim, as a friend, really feel good about it? Or did he envy my luck?" "And was Paul friendly just because I had a car?" When we look back, doubts like these can make us feel bad.

But when we look back, it is too late.

Why do we go wrong about our friends, or our enemies? Sometimes what people say hides their real meanings. And if we do not really listen, we miss the feeling behind the words. Suppose someone tells you, "You're a lucky dog!" Is he really on your side? If he says, "You're a lucky guy!" that is being friendly. But "a lucky dog?" There is a bit of envy in those words. What he may be saying is that he does not think you deserve your luck.

"Just think of all the things you have to be thankful for" is another phrase that says one thing and means another. It could mean that the speaker is trying to get you to see your problem. But this phrase contains the thought that your problem is not at all important.

How can you tell the real meaning behind someone's words? One way is to take a good look at the person talking. Do his words fit the way he looks? Is what he says shown by the tone of voice? The look in his eyes? Stop and think. The minute you spend thinking about the real meaning of what people say to you may save your another mistake.

8. Knowing about yourself means not only that you find what you are good at and what you like, it also means discovering what you are not good at and what you don't like. Both help you to see your aim in life.

Although most students would be unhappy if they found that they had failed an advanced math course, they have actually learned a great deal about themselves. They know they should not become engineers or physical scientist, and that they should not be good at accounting work. So failing can help a student to lead a much happier life he or she draws the right conclusion from the failing. They may then decide on their aim and choose the kind of work they would like to do.

It is impossible to decide whether or not you like something until you have tried it. If you decide that you would like to play the violin, you need to take more than one lesson before you can know whether you have any interest or ability.

It's not enough to want to be a violinist. You also have to like the hard and long training before you become one. If you would enjoy being a great violinist but hate the work, forget it.

It's a good plan to try as many as possible when you are still young. And then you will come to a wise decision.

二、下面各段没有主题句，请根据全段内容写出一个主题句。

1. For example teachers live selling knowledge, philosophers by selling wisdom and priests by selling spiritual comfort. Though it may be possible to measure the value of material goods in terms of money, it is very difficult to calculate the true value of services which people perform for us. The conditions of society are such that sills have to be paid for in the same way that goods are paid for at shop. Everyone has something to sell.

2. Before entering a house in Japan, it is good manners to take off your shoes. In European countries even though shoes sometimes become very muddy, this is not done. A guest in a Chinese house never finishes a drink. He leaves a little to show that he has had enough. In a Malaysian house, too, a guest leaves a little food. In England, a guest always finishes a drink to show that he has enjoyed it. It seems that manners in different countries are never the same.

第二节　支撑句和结尾句

在主题句确立以后就需要具体的事例、数据等对段落的主题进行叙述、论述或说明以支撑主题论点。这些句子就是支撑句（supporting sentence），有些地方也叫拓展句、支持句。支撑句要围绕主题句展开，服从于主题句，不能走题。支撑句可以是几件事、几个数据，也可以是一件事或一个数据。

一个支撑句论述主题的某一个侧面，多个支撑句对主题形成多视角、多维度的支撑。

支撑句应该言简意赅，不讲与主题句不相关的话，要突出重点，直奔主题。结尾句就是在前期论证的基础上总结全段，得出结论，与主题句遥相呼应，结束全段。少数段落中也可以不写结尾句（concluding sentence）。

支撑句可以通过多种方法实现，常见的有举例、列举、递进、因果、比较和对照等手法，在实际写作中往往是几种方法结合使用，更能充分支撑主题，论证充分，写出的段落更有说服力。

一、举例法

用具有典型意义的个别事例来论证主题句叫举例法。举例法常用的连接词有：for example, for instance, to illustrate, in general, in particular, specifically, generally, especially, occasionally, such as, namely…

【范文】

Friends make a difference to people's life. For example, the mother of the great thinker and philosopher Mencius in ancient China moved to three different places to live in order to be with good neighbors. Being with good neighbors and making friends who were hardworking paved the way for the little boy to become a great man in history. Karl Marx and Friedrich Engels became life-long friends after they first met in Paris. They wrote the famous book *The Capital* in collaboration. So, it's important to make good friends who are positive and optimistic.

二、列举法

列举法是列举若干事例，逐一陈述，最后得出合乎逻辑的结论，对主题句进行支撑。列举法因为要列举一系列的事实、事例，常会用到一些连接词，常用的连接词如下：

To start with/Second/And third; Firstly/Secondly/And last/Finally; first/second/third/next; for one thing, for another; on one hand, on the other hand;

also, then, in addition, moreover, furthermore, besides, additionally, likewise, in the same way...

【范文】

Playing mobile phones in class has negative impacts on your studies. First, you cannot concentrate on your lessons. Second, your behaviors distract your deskmate's attentiveness on what the teacher is saying. Third, being exposed to earphones for long hours does harm to your hearing. Last but not least, it makes the teacher annoyed and he may not let you pass the exam.

三、递进法

递进法是围绕主题句逐步展开，层层递进，论证逐步加深的写作方法。递进法常见的关联词有：furthermore, moreover, besides, what's more等。

【范文】

Smoking should be prohibited. As we all know smoking does bad to people's health. Besides the fact that it pollutes the air, smoking annoys people around you. What's more, second-hand smoking is even more harmful to your friends and family members. A smoker is not welcomed anywhere. So, people should give up smoking.

四、因果法

因果法就是紧扣主题句说明主题中的事件发生的原因和结果。常见的关联词有for, because, since, owing to, due to, as a result of, because of, therefore, thus, accordingly, consequently, on account of, because, as, since, now that, result in, result from, lead to, contribute to, as a result/consequence, accordingly, for this reason等。常用的句型有There are…reasons for… The reason for…is that/ lies in the fact that…等。

【范文】

Air flights are often delayed and some of them are even cancelled recently. This is because Spring Festival is drawing near, busiest season of the year for transportation in China is being with us again. To make it worse, some northern provinces are having big snows ever seen in history. Flights are stopped due to bad weather. As a result, many passengers are stopped at airports. They need water and food. But most important of all, they want to go home.

五、比较与对比法

此方法用来说明相同点和不同点。可以逐项对比，也可以整体论述后再对比。常用连接词有：

On the one hand…On the other hand…

For one thing…for another…

On the contrary, In/By contrast, just as, likewise, in much the same way…

Compare to/with, in comparison to/with, instead, nevertheless/however, in spite of…

Whereas, even if/though, but, while…

【范文】

Travelling in E.U., you find everything exotic but exciting. It's very easy to tell a Chinese from a European. Our skin is yellow while they are white, we have black hair and black eyes while theirs blonde and blue. Chinese people like to gather together and tend to talk loudly, but the Europeans are quieter and prefer to stay alone. However, we share many things that are very human in spite of all the differences we have, we all like peace and want to be helpful to people who live in poverty around the world.

六、问题法

问题法在段首描述并设置一个问题作为主题，然后在支撑句中陈述自己的观点、方法，并展开论证。问题法通常用于议论文的写作中。

总之，支撑句就是为了说明主题句中的论点、论证主题句中的观点，使主题句更加丰满，使段落有血肉，具有说服力、感染力。

练习题

一、给下列的主题句写若干个支撑句。

1. Chinese people are shy.

2. Reading does good to your English study.

3. I love travelling.

4. It's important to memorize more English words.

二、按照下列主题句，写一个完整的段落。

1. I love dogs.

2. I like our college.

3. We should not talk in class.

4. Too much use of mobile phones is harmful.

三、完成下列段落。

1. I like _____. First, because _____. Second, _____. Third, _____. So, _____.

2. Last Sunday, I _____. I _____.
We _____ and _____.
We _____.

3. My pet _____. Its _____. It is _____. Do you _____?

4. I prefer _____ to _____. Because, _____. The next reason, I _____. The most important of all _____.

5. You don't have to be a top student in class to be successful. The great _____ and he _____. Later, _____. From this story, _____.

第二章 写好一个段落

一个好的段落不应该是一连串句子的堆砌。除了句子本身须紧扣主题外，一个好的段落应该遵循以下几个原则，即一致性（unity）、条理性（order）、连贯性（coherence）和完整性（completeness）。

第一节 段落的一致性

段落的一致性是指所有的支撑句必须围绕主题句展开，陈述对象要一致，整段写作风格要保持一致，不能一会儿使用书面语一会儿使用口头语；与主题无关的句子哪怕再优美，再能体现作者的英文水平都应该舍弃，同时支撑句中不能掺杂与主题无关的信息。下面以范文说明。

【范文一】

（1）Many students fail coming to classes without any reasons nowadays. （2）In my opinion, playing truant is harmful to students' studies. （3）A student's main task in a school is to learn. （4）Our teachers prepare the lessons very carefully and they deserve our respect and we are obliged to go to their classes. （5）One may say that food in the canteen is bad and the price is high. So what? That doesn't justify your misdeeds in avoiding classes. （6）Most important thing is that you will not pass the exams if you miss too many classes. （7）So, let's get up earlier and go to classes!

【修改意见】

本段是一篇迷你议论文，以提出现象开始全段。本段的主题句是第二句In my opinion, playing truant is harmful to students' studies。本文除第五句外，都能紧扣这个主题。所以，即使第五句写得妙笔生花，也要忍痛割爱，予以删除。

【修改后】

Many students fail coming to classes without any reasons nowadays.（1）In my opinion, skipping classes is harmful to students' studies.（2）A student's main task in a school is to learn.（3）Our teachers prepare the lessons very carefully and they deserve our respect and we are obliged to go to their classes.（4）Most important thing is that you will not pass the exams if you miss too many classes.（5）So, let's get up earlier and go to classes!

【范文二】

（1）Sunday is my favorite day of the week.（2）I like it because on Sunday, I watch football.（3）On other days, I also get to watch football but not all day. There are other sports on other days to watch on TV.（4）Sunday lunch is a favorite of mine because I eat with my father in front of the TV.（5）All the other days, I have to eat at the table which is less fun.（6）Some days my dad doesn't make it home from work until after I'm in bed.（7）Some weeks my dad travels, and I don't see him for several days.（8）The highlight of the day is when we watch the Dolphins play.（9）Dad and I get so excited, we yell and cheer together. （10）The thing that I like to do best in the world is watch TV with my dad.

【修改意见】

本段落主题是星期天是我最喜欢的一天，本意想写作者喜欢星期天，喜欢星期天和爸爸待在一起的美好时光。但是由于无关的句子太多，重点被稀释，读者的注意力被分散，主题被湮灭在无关的信息里面了。因此，建议删除第三、五、六、七句。

【修改后】

Sunday is my favorite day because I spend the day watching football with my dad. On Sunday, unlike the other days of the week when he works, my dad spends the whole day with me watching football on TV. We even eat lunch together while watching. The highlight of the day is watching the Dolphins Game. Dad and I get so excited, we yell and cheer together. On Sundays, I get to combine watching my favorite sport and spending time with my favorite person—what a great day!

15

第二节　段落的连贯性

段落的连贯性通常指两种情况。第一种情况是逻辑上的连贯又叫"意连"，它是内在的连续性，不一定体现在字里行间，如"Jim is a freshman in our university, his major is English Education, we all like him."本句中的his, him都与Jim有内在逻辑上的连贯，如果说成her major is English Education, we all like her那么描写的就不是Jim了，性别就不一致了。第二种情况是句子与句子之间的连贯。这种连贯又叫"形连"，它指句子与句子之间的过渡自然、流畅，意义上紧密衔接，让读者感到事件、情节、论点交代清楚，有条不紊。为了达到连贯通常需要使用帮助过渡的接续词或转折词。

【范文一】

Nowadays more and more students order takeouts and enjoy delivery-at-door service. But I never eat take-away food and often persuade my classmates not to buy any. On the one hand, it's not safe to buy food you never know who made it and what it was made from. On the other hand, takeout food is usually more expensive than that in the canteen. Moreover, used foam-containers and plastic bags are littered here and there in the dormitory, which is public space shared by your roommates. They smell terrible if not disposed of right after eating. Flies and rats can often be seen in dorms where they buy takeouts. This may cause diseases.

【点评】

本段落主题是我不点外卖。从第三句开始为扩展句部分用以支撑主题，为了使段落显得连贯，本段落使用了on the one hand, on the other hand, moreover 等接续词，使全段行文读起来流畅连贯，一气呵成，读者很容易把握作者想要表达的观点，有较强的说服力。

【范文二】

（1）Cheating in exams should be punished.（2）First, if you cheat in the exams, it's unfair for students who work hard at their lessons.（3）Second, you miss the chance to be corrected by the teachers because they think you are doing quite well in the courses.（4）Third, the teachers are so watchful when supervising an exam and never give you a chance. (5) Fine scores are very important to apply for a scholarship. (6) Last but not least, why not spend more time on your studies since you have so much time to prepare for the cheating?

【点评】

本段落的主题是考试作弊应该受到应有的惩罚。第二句和第三句能围绕主题叙事，展开议论；第四句走题了，监考教师考试严格不严格与本段主题无明显关联；第五句走题，没有说明申请奖学金与作弊之间的关系；最后一句是一句不错的结尾句。

【修改后】

Cheating in exams should be punished. First, if you cheat in the exams, it's unfair for students who work hard at their lessons. Second, you miss the chance to be corrected by the teachers because they think you are doing quite well in the courses. Third, you lose the chance to apply for the scholarship according to the regulations. Everybody wants fine scores but honesty is more important than anything else. Last, why not spend more time on your studies since you have so much time to prepare for the cheating?

第三节　段落的条理性

主题句确立以后，就要思考怎么写支撑句，支撑句以不少于三句为宜。在紧扣主题的前提下，根据自己的写作内容，按照主次、时间先后、一般具体等因素，合理安排句子的顺序，不能杂乱无章、先后不分、主次颠倒，总之要符合一定的逻辑顺序，让读者感到自然有序，情节发展环环相扣，人物描写细腻，观点明朗，关系明确，思路清晰明了。

通常情况下，叙述性的段落以事件情节发展的时间先后排序或以空间场景变化的先后顺序排列，将事件发展的客观过程展现给读者；说明性的段落宜采用由远及近、从外到内、由上到下的顺序排列；议论性的段落一般按主次轻重、由表及里、由浅入深、由因及果、由现象到本质、由具体到概括、由感性到理性的逻辑顺序展开。

　　一个段落内的句子安排遵循如下几种顺序：时间顺序（Time Order or Chronological Order）、位置或空间顺序（Space Order or Spatial Order）和逻辑顺序（Logical Order）。下面分别说明。

一、时间顺序

　　记叙事件发展经过的段落，支撑句通常采用时间顺序。这样的安排使读者感到条理分明，叙事清楚，读者沿着时间轴一步步了解整个事件的发生、发展过程，从而达到完美的写作效果。

【范文一】

（1）The first day I was at college was wonderful.（2）Our train arrived at the station late in the morning and we were received by the volunteers warmly.（3）We talked cheerfully about life on campus and of course, the local food on the bus on the way back to the college.（4）We arrived at the college about fifteen minutes later and got a warm welcome once again.（5）We did all those things for registration helped by volunteers there.（6）When I got into our dormitory I was a little tired but excited.

【点评】

　　本段落基本上使用简单句和并列句完成。第一句为主题句，主题就是大学报到第一天的见闻和经历；第二至第五句为支撑句；第六句是结尾句。从第二句开始即按照时间发展顺序排列，从到达火车站、报名注册、安排到宿舍，整个过程叙事清楚，思路明确，读者犹如身临其境，对大学校园生活充满向往。

【范文二】

Day gave way to the night at about 7:00 and Jim started out for the dinner with his girlfriend. About fifteen minutes later after they got on the main road, their car jolted a little as if running over something... The banquet went in a pleasant atmosphere and all the guests were very satisfied at the end of the dinner. Jim got into his car and went back home. He sat down on the sofa and turned on

TV; local evening news was going on and he heard one old man was hit dead by a blue Rolls-Royce with the driver fleeing the scene and the hit-and-run guy was wanted by the police… Trembling, Jim took up his cellphone and dialed the number of the police.

【点评】

本段记叙了一个小故事，整个段落以时间顺序安排情节的发展。作者提及了几个重要的时间节点，即七点钟出门，七点一刻他开车上了主路，在没有察觉的情况下出了一个交通事故，宴会后到家看电视才知道自己闯下了大祸。故事的叙述通常都是以时间轴安排情节发展的，本文作者以时间为主要线索讲述主人公当天晚上的活动，详写了出门上路，宴会不是主要叙述内容，所以寥寥数笔一带而过，大量的笔墨用在了主人公Jim回到家以后看到电视的心理活动：撞人逃逸是重罪，作者经过激烈的内心斗争决定向警察自首。本文完美地讲述了一个不幸的车祸故事。

二、位置或空间顺序

按照位置或空间顺序的变化来组织一个段落，一般用在记叙性段落里，可用于不希望用时间顺序来叙述事件的发展过程或者时间概念比较模糊或者时间顺序不重要的情况。空间顺序一般有从上到下、由远及近、由外向内及其他排列方法。在以位置或空间顺序叙述事件的时候还可以采用插叙、倒叙等写作技巧，我们在初学阶段不提倡使用。

【范文】

（1）Uncle Wang took us on a visit to the Great Hall of the People today. （2）From far away, the great pillars and national emblem shone in brightness. （3）We found ourselves in the Central Hall just through the grand entrance with chandeliers hanging from the ceiling and saw so many rows of seats in meeting halls. （4）We were interested in everything we saw. （5）On stepping out of the Great Hall, we headed north for the Banquet Hall which can house thousands of people at dinner. （6）I was awed by the solemnity and grandeur of the Great Hall of the People.

【点评】

本段落描写的是一名小学生参观人民大会堂的经过。全段共六句，第一句为主题句，第二至第五句为支撑句。第二至四句描述过程为由远及近，远远地看到十一根巨大的大理石柱及国徽在阳光中熠熠生辉，闪着光芒。由外及里，我们穿过大厅走进礼堂，看到巨大的吊灯和无数座位。第五句由场景顺序变化带领读者继续探访，来到大会堂宴会厅。第六句为结尾句，参观了庄严肃穆的人民大会堂，崇敬之情油然而生。全段一气呵成，读者随着场景的转换，和作者一道参观了雄伟壮观的人民大会堂。

三、逻辑顺序

段落的逻辑顺序通常分为三种，即主次顺序、从一般到具体及从具体到一般。语句的逻辑顺序关系到整个段落的连贯，属于前面所说的意连。

（一）主次顺序

主次顺序指按照事物的重要性程度安排叙事先后。

【范文一】

（1）Nowadays more and more young people stay single when they reach the age they are supposed to get married.（2）One of the reasons for this is that they are busy with their work and can spare no time caring about their own business.（3）Another reason that delays them in marriage may be that it's hard to find someone that you really love.（4）A third reason for reluctance in falling in love with someone is due to the high price of houses in cosmopolitan cities and high bride price.（5）In a word, they are not well-prepared for marriages.

【点评】

本段落主题是越来越多的年轻人选择不结婚或不愿找对象。第二句至第四句为支撑句，这三个句子排列的顺序遵循了主次原则，事业心强工作忙是找不到对象的最主要原因，其次是没有合适的，再次是大城市的高额房价让年轻人在这里安家的想法可望而不可即，彩礼太高也是找不到结婚对象的一个因素。最后一句是结尾句，年轻人还没有准备好，可以宽容一点，让其继续准备。总体上看，语句安排合理，层层递进，主次分明，观点明确，分析了年轻人现在婚姻的难点痛点，没有一句废话，具有较强的说服力。

【范文二】

（1）I enjoy reading.（2）Books are a good past-time when I feel bored.（3）Of all the books I love stories about Chinese Kungfu and thrillers most.（4）Besides, we can learn many things we didn't know before by reading books written by great philosophers.（5）We know more by inheriting wisdom of our forefathers by reading.（6）We feel happy because we learn something in every book we read.（7）If I have seen further it is by standing on the shoulders of giants.

【点评】

本段的主题是我爱读书，注意用词是enjoy不是like，表达出了因为读书而内心愉悦的心情，不是喜欢读书的动作。上文中第二至第六句为支撑句，写喜欢阅读的原因，但是主次安排十分不合理。读小说虽然也是读书但不能算是我们所理解的阅读，而应该是消遣，是一个非常次要的细节，放在首位显然与整体格调不匹配，弱化了主题。因此，有必要对支撑句的顺序和细节进行调整和删减。

【修改后】

I enjoy reading. Books are a bridge that leads us to the vast ocean of human knowledge. We inherit wisdom of the mankind by reading. We feel happy because we learn something in every book we read. Sometimes I also read stories by great writers when I feel bored. Issac Newton was once heard to say "If I have seen further it is by standing on the shoulders of Giants." That's why I enjoy reading.

（二）从一般到具体

从一般到具体指的是从事物的普遍性入手，然后以个别事物为落点的写作手法。既然是普遍性或一般性肯定是高度概括、抽象的一般性原则或者是人们的共识，如英语里经常用到的开始句As we all know… As is known to all…但是过于概括难免过于空洞无物，还需要使其具体化。

【范文】

Many people like Chinese food. Of all of them, I like hotpot best for its superb flavor and its spiciness. You may make a hotpot at home or order one in a restaurant. It's extremely convenient to make a hotpot, you get started just by putting all the ingredients you fancy to eat into the pot. Hotpot food in a restaurant may be more original. People like to eat hot-pot food especially on winter days because it keeps you warm. Hotpot food is winning more and more popularity around the world.

【点评】

本段主题写我喜欢火锅。作者先从人们都喜欢中餐说起，这是一个具有普遍性的共识。从第二句开始过渡到在所有中餐中我最喜欢火锅，完美演绎了从一般到具体的写作思路。

（三）从具体到一般

从具体到一般通常是为了说明某个道理，先从具体事例开始，经过列举事实、分析案例、演绎推理，得出一般性规律，目的是说服读者，多用于议论文或说明文中。

【范文】

One evening, a butcher was going back home after finishing the day's business. In his baskets were only some bones left over. To his horror, he suddenly noticed two wolves following half way. He stopped to defend himself with his back to a pile of straw. So they stared at one another for some time. Then one of the wolves seemed bored of this and went away while the other was dozing away lasily. All of a sudden, the butcher heard some strange sound behind himself in the pile, he walked around it and saw one wolf busy digging through the straw meaning to assault him from the back. The butcher was quick and killed the wolf with his sword. Wolves are cunning, but human beings always outwit them.

【点评】

本段是中学语文课本里的一篇文言文小说。整个段落以紧张的气氛讲述了一个惊心动魄的人狼大战的故事，从尾随、对峙，到一狼试图从屠夫背后发动突袭，人与狼之间斗智斗勇，但是终究人类智高一筹，完胜两狼。本段从具体事例入手，最后得出结论：再狡猾的狼也不是人类的对手，是比较经典的从具体到一般的记叙性小文章。

练习题

一、将下列句子重新排序，使之成为一个通顺的段落。

1. And if I'm really late, I even miss the school bus.

2. If I forget to set my alarm, I get up late and rush through everything.

3. As a result, I often have to gulp my breakfast.

4. It's always much better if I remember to set the alarm, so I have more time to get ready.

5. I also might rush out and forget my books.

二、从下列所给的词语中选择合适的转换词填入括号内。

1

---
but recently, initially, later, in the eighteenth century

People's idea of what popular music actually is has changed over the years since the term was first coined. _____ , the phrase "popular music" simply meant music that had become more available to the public. _____ , the appearance of inexpensive sheet music meant that amateur and family musicians could play at home or in local gatherings. But _____ , with the advent of recording equipment and the gramophone player, these amateur musicians slowly become professionals in their own right. "Popular music" then referred only to music that become public through the growing recording industry, which had a monopoly on deciding whose music got heard. _____ , with the introduction of digital do-it-yourself computer programs, popular music is once again returning to its original meaning: music made by the wider amateur public.

2

---
but, for example, first, and finally, this, also

Though baseball players use less equipment than players in many other sports, they still need certain basics to play the game safely and well. _____ , of course, each player needs a bat and glove. This personal equipment allows players to play positions in the diamond or out on the field, but also lets them come up to bat. _____ players may _____ need more specialized safety equipment, depending on their position. _____ , when batting, they wear a helmet to protect against being hit with the ball, and may wear shin or arm guards as well. _____ , catchers wear specialized masks, chest protectors, and shin guards. Using the right equipment is just as important in baseball as in any other sport.

3

then, first, this calculation, finally, early

My family always throws the best New Year's Eve party, and people love coming to it each year. We start _____ with our plans, to be sure everything is ready on time. _____ , we make a basic guest list, and then double that number of people because we always welcome extras. _____ helps us get an idea of how many supplies we'll need. we start stocking up, at least two months ahead of time. We begin making goodies that can go in the freezer sometime late in November. _____ , a few days before December 31, we start putting up decorations, adding chairs and small tables, and preparing last minute food. When party time arrives, we're just as free as our guests to have a great time and properly usher in the new year.

三、下列段落有个别语句不符合一致性原则，请找出来。

（1）I hate being pressed for blind dates. （2）I stay single till now after I graduated from college many years ago. （3）In recent years, whenever my mom calls she would tell me to find a boyfriend as soon as possible. （4）She often goes travelling around the country and buys me a lot of presents. （5）What's more, she plays an active role in finding boyfriends for me and bombards me with such words as "This guy got married and they had a baby last month…that girl married a rich man and went abroad…and so on, and so on…" （6）During the New Year

Holiday, she always forces me to meet those boys for blind dates. (7) But what idea I hold on to is always that forced marriages result in no happy life. (8) Now, I am afraid of going back home.

四、分析下列段落是如何实现连贯性的。

(1) The human body is a wonderful piece of work that nature has created. (2) It is not beautiful like the body of a butterfly or peacock but it is shaped practically. (3) It can do many types of work which other animals cannot. (4) It is not strong like the body of a tiger. (5) But in place of physical strength it has a big and sharp brain. (6) By using this brain the human physique has been able to overcome many of its limitations. (7) By sitting in an aeroplane it flies faster than a kite, by riding a motorcycle it travels faster than a leopard, and by firing a machine gun it fights much better than a tiger. (8) In spite of all this, the human body suffers from many diseases because it has a weakness for habits such as smoking, drinking and overeating. (9) When it is healthy the body can give great pleasure but when it is sick it can cause great pain. (10) The wise man would always keep his body fit because a healthy mind can work only in a healthy body.

第三章　提纲的撰写

英语写作分为命题写作与非命题写作。命题写作就是老师命题，学生完成写作任务。非命题写作，就是给一个写作范围，学生根据自己对该范围的理解，从自己的知识能力出发自我命题。命题范围在英语里叫prompt，它的本意是写作提示，相当于语文老师说的写作范围。自由撰稿人常常自己确定写作范围，并自我命题。科研报告、学术论文也属于自我命题。学术论文写作不属于我们的探讨范围，故在此不作介绍。

在写作计划确立之后，就要进行创作前的准备工作。通常情况下，英语写作分为如下步骤，即头脑风暴（brainstorming）、撰写提纲（outlining）、草稿（drafting）、修改与编辑（revising/editing）及校对（proofreading）等步骤。头脑风暴具体做法主要有发散联想法（freewriting）、列问题清单法（question listing）和图示导引法（mapping/concept map）等。由于中外文化、思维方式和教育思想上的差异，有些做法不一定适合照搬过来为我所用，在此只作一个简单的介绍，供同学们参考，这里我们主要学习提纲撰写（outlining），对以后读研阶段的论文创作或有裨益。

第一节　预写与构思

初学写作基本上都是命题作文。拿到题目后首先要做的自然是进行深思熟虑进而形成基本思路，如果时间充足，可以自行查阅资料。如果时间受限，如在写作考试中，必须在一定时间内完成，又没有现成的资料可以查阅，这时自己平时在大脑中储备的知识就显得尤为有用。此时要做的就是要积极调动已经掌握的与题目相关的知识，激活大脑，让思路在大脑中逐渐形成，进而再形成文字。

头脑风暴是调动大脑中已经储备的知识以及自己的生活经历，进而形成写作思路的一种有效的构思方法。写作中的头脑风暴概念与其他地方说的含义不完全相同：课堂上引入一个新概念的时候进行的头脑风暴，是要大家群策群力、共同探讨，一起挖掘出与话题相关的所有信息，使大家在集思广益的基础上对该话题有一个全面、充分的了解。写作中的头脑风暴主要依靠个人的独立思考，调动自己大脑中已经存在的信息，进而形成写作思路，并在此基础上整理出符合一致性、条理性、连贯性和完整性四原则的逻辑脉络清楚、主题鲜明的提纲。头脑风暴主要有以下几种方法。

一、发散联想法

发散联想法（freewriting）就是围绕所拟定的主题，打开思路，自由发挥，不考虑文章结构，不考虑条理与连贯，把能想到的与主题相关的思想、观点、词汇全部都写出来，说是"胡言乱语"并不为过。在后期的正式写作中，可以从中发现有价值的线索，把它们组织进文章的相关段落中，使之成为文章有机的一部分。

二、列问题清单法

列问题清单法（question listing）是将与主题相关的方方面面的观点尽可能多地以问题形式罗列出来，然后做出客观的简要回答。列问题清单的好处是能够直接、简明地体现出各个侧面与主题的逻辑联系和因果关系，为写作者提示若干思路和可能的写作方向。同时，它能帮助作者跳出思维局限性，防止卡在某一个局部的小问题上思维短路，以全局视角和高度考虑通篇，从而保证思维的流畅，确保写作顺利进行。例如：

Who cheats in exams?	Some students.
Why do they cheat?	For better scores.

Who is unfavorably influenced?	The teacher and the hard-working students.
What to do about this?	To be punished.

三、图示导引法

图示导引法很像现在十分流行的思维导图。它的做法是将你所能想到的可能应该出现在段落中的事物、情节以图示的形式，用几条线连接起来，有助于作者明确思路和逻辑关系。看着图示再根据自己的需要取舍，有的线索要增加，不需要的线索则可以予以删除。在大脑中建立了这种形象思维的逻辑联系之后，就可以着手撰写提纲了。

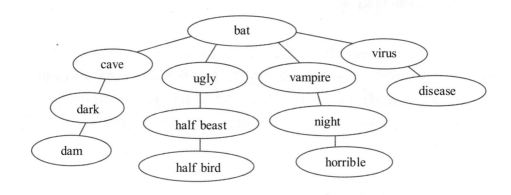

第二节　撰写提纲

写作提纲是一篇文章的基本框架和总体设计。英语的写作提纲对全文其他段落具有规定性和提示性。在主题已经明确的前提下，写作提纲决定着文章从哪些侧面丰富主题、有多少段落、每个段落顺序怎么安排，以及哪些段落详写哪些段落略写。同时，它对于写作思路和内容有提示的作用。提纲之于文章犹如设计图纸之于楼房的建筑。没有提纲写出的文章随意性强，叙述、论述没有整体意识，文章结构没有总体安排，各段落很难达到从属于主题、服务于主题的目的，其结果必然影响全文的整体效果，影响说理的逻辑性、叙事的连贯性以及说明的系统全面性。一个好的写作提纲基本上就是一篇文章的雏形，它奠定了整篇文章的架构。

一、提纲的组成

规范的英语写作提纲由三个部分组成，即引言段（introduction/introductory paragraph）、正文（body）和结尾段（conclusion/concluding paragraph）。主题思想（thesis）需要在引言段中表达出来，表达主题的句子叫中心思想句（thesis statement），后面的段落都要围绕这个中心思想去写。由于正文部分的所有段落都是对主题的支撑所以也称为支撑段。各段之间逻辑上要连续，内容要符合一致性（unity）、条理性（order）、连贯性（coherence）原则。文章需要有一个结尾段落以保证其具有完整性，结尾段是对中心思想句的总结、综述，但不是对主题思想句的简单重复，而是在前几段论述基础上的一个升华，要达到一个新的境界。撰写提纲要做到以下几点：

（1）确立文章的中心思想。

（2）围绕这个中心思想展开叙述、论述。如果是议论文，其论据观点越明确、范围越小，文章越能紧扣主题。

（3）确保每个段落的一级标题能从不同的侧面支撑全文的主题。

（4）确保每个一级标题都能得到二级标题的支撑。

（5）每段一级标题句下创建至少两个二级标题句。如果找不出两个以上的二级标题句，说明这个一级标题句与全文主题相关性不强，需要更换一个关联性更强的一级标题句。

英语文章的经典样式为五段式，包括引言段、正文部分三段和结尾段。每段结束时下一段另起一行，每个段首单词需要缩进两个字符（缩进在提纲里无法体现出来，在文章写作的时候必须遵循）。

1	Introductory paragraph

2	Body Paragraph 1
3	Body Paragraph 2
4	Body Paragraph 3
5	Concluding paragraph

为方便初学者，也可以把正文部分简化成三段式。

1	Introductory paragraph
2	Body paragraph
3	Concluding paragraph

二、提纲的格式

无论五段式还是三段式，英语写作提纲的布局（layout）需要遵守一定的规范格式。其标记形式如下：

第一层一级标题句采用大写的罗马数字标注，如Roman numerals（Ⅰ，Ⅱ，Ⅲ，Ⅳ，Ⅴ, etc.）

第二层二级标题句采用大写英文字母标注，如upper case letters（A, B, C, etc.）

第三层三级标题句采用阿拉伯数字标注，如Arabic numerals（1, 2, 3, etc.）

第四层四级标题句采用英文小写字母标注，如lower case letters（a, b, c, etc.）

第五层五级标题句采用小写罗马数字标注，如 lower case Roman numerals（i, ii, iii, iv, v, etc.）

这种提纲模式广泛应用于英语写作实践中，学术文章、毕业论文的写作提纲也采用这种标记方式。

Ⅰ. Introduction:

A. General information about topic, reason for reader to be interested, context, etc.

B. Thesis statement

Ⅱ. Body Paragraph 1

A. Topic Sentence

B. Supporting Sentence 1 (example, data, explanation,etc.)

1. Detail/example/etc.

2. Detail/example/etc.

a. Detail/example/etc.

b. Detail/example/etc.

C. Supporting Sentence 2 (example, data, explanation,etc.)

1. Detail/example/etc.

2. Detail/example/etc.

a. Detail/example/etc.

b. Detail/example/etc.

D. Supporting Sentence 3 (example, data, explanation,etc.)

1. Detail/example/etc.

2. Detail/example/etc.

a. Detail/example/etc.

b. Detail/example/etc.

Ⅲ. Body Paragraph 2

A. Topic Sentence

B. Supporting Sentence 1 (example, data, explanation,etc.)

1. Detail/example/etc.

2. Detail/example/etc.

a. Detail/example/etc.

b. Detail/example/etc.

C. Supporting Sentence 2(example, data, explanation,etc.)

1. Detail/example/etc.

2. Detail/example/etc.

a. Detail/example/etc.

b. Detail/example/etc.

D. Supporting Sentence 3 (example, data, explanation,etc.)

1. Detail/example/etc.

2. Detail/example/etc.

a. Detail/example/etc.

b. Detail/example/etc.

Ⅳ. Body Paragraph 3

A. Topic Sentence

B. Supporting Sentence 1 (example, data, explanation,etc.)

1. Detail/example/etc.

2. Detail/example/etc.

a. Detail/example/etc.

b. Detail/example/etc.

C. Supporting Sentence 2 (example, data, explanation,etc.)

1. Detail/example/etc.

2. Detail/example/etc.

a. Detail/example/etc.

b. Detail/example/etc.

D. Supporting Sentence 3 (example, data, explanation,etc.)

1. Detail/example/etc.

2. Detail/example/etc.

a. Detail/example/etc.

b. Detail/example/etc.

Ⅴ. Concluding Paragraph

A. Summary of main points, return to general context, wrap-up of essay, etc.

B. Re-state thesis

需要注意的是，英语写作提纲的编写中同一层级要遵循逻辑内容对等和表达形式对称的原则，即：

（1）同一层级的内容必须是对等的。

（2）同一层级的标题句形式上应由互为平行、对称的单词、短语、句子组成或表达形式具有对称的句型和语法结构。例如：

【例1】

Ⅰ. Sichuan Food

Ⅱ. Guangdong Food

本例中，不能直接把火锅列为一级标题，因为火锅属于川菜下面的一种，与粤菜大类不对等。

【例2】

Ⅰ. To travel or to stay at home during the vacation

Ⅱ. I would like to go to Tibet

例2中，一级标题内容不对等，句子形式不对称。当然这种形式上的对称也不是绝对的，如标题—句式混合标题中，就不需要遵守对称性原则。

三、提纲的三种形式

英语的写作提纲通常有三种形式，它们是：

（1）句子式提纲（Sentence Outline）

（2）标题式提纲（Topic Outline）

（3）标题—句子式混合提纲（Topic-sentence Outline）

以下分别介绍。

（一）句子式提纲

句子式提纲中，每一个层级的提纲内容都是一个完整的句子。在后面的写作中，有些句子可以拿来即用。

【例1】

Life in the Country

Ⅰ. Introduction

Provide background story about urban life and that in the rural area.

Thesis Statement: I prefer life in the country to that in a city if I were to choose.

Ⅱ. Life in the country

A. The scenery is good, the water is clean and the air is fresh.

B. You can take a walk in the trees and fish in the rivers.

C. The people there are friendly.

D. It's quieter in the country and you have more time to think over things.

Ⅲ. Life in the city, a comparison

A. You are Stressed-out and always busy with work to make money to make ends meet.

B. It is noisy in a city and the air is polluted.

C. The city is crowded with no good scenery, you have nowhere to go to relax yourself.

Ⅳ. Conclusion

A. Life in the country is quiet and peaceful and is fast changing.

B. We need to make money to support ourselves in the city, but still enjoying staying in the country now and then for a refresh and for new inspirations in life.

【例2】

Why The School Year Should be Shorter

Ⅰ. Introduction

A. Introduce the primary argument or main point of your essay using a thesis statement and context.

B. Thesis: The school year is too long, and should be shortened to benefit students and teachers, save district money, and improve test scores and academic results. Other countries have shorter school years, and achieve better results.

Ⅱ. Body Paragraph 1

A. Describe the primary argument and provide supporting details and evidence.

1. Topic Sentence: A shorter school year would benefit students and teachers by giving them more time off.

2. Detail Sentence 1: Students and teachers would be able to spend more time with their families.

3. Detail Sentence 2: Teachers would be refreshed and rejuvenated and able to teach more effectively.

Ⅲ. Body Paragraph 2

A. Provide additional supporting details and evidence.

B. Topic Sentence: A shorter school year would save school districts millions of dollars per year.

C. Detail Sentence 1: Districts could save money on energy costs by keeping schools closed longer.

D. Detail Sentence 2: A shorter school year means much lower supply and transportation costs.

E. Detail Sentence 3: Well-rested and happy students would help improve test scores.

Ⅳ. Body Paragraph 3

A. Provide additional or supplemental supporting details, evidence, and analysis.

B. Topic Sentence: Shortening the school year would also provide many benefits for parents and caregivers.

C. Detail Sentence 1: A shorter school year would mean less stress and running around for parents.

D. Detail Sentence 2: Caregivers would have more balance in their lives with fewer days in the school year.

V. Conclusion

A. Conclude the essay with an overview of the main argument, and highlight the importance of your evidence and conclusion.

B. Concluding Sentence: Shortening the school year would be a great way to improve the quality of life for students, teachers, and parents while saving money for districts and improving academic results.

（二）标题式提纲

标题式提纲，每个层级的内容不需要是一个完整的句子，它可以是若干单词、短语，对每个段落的写作具有强烈的提示性。

【例1】

Nature vs. Nurture

Ⅰ. Introduction

A. Background information

B. Arguments you will explain within the body

C. Thesis statement

Ⅱ. Body Paragraph 1

A. Nature

B. Genetic makeup

C. Predisposition is not destiny

D. Just because someone has a talent, doesn't mean that they will be good right away

Ⅲ. Body Paragraph 2

A. Nurture

B. The role of environment

C. Parents give their children the best environment

Ⅳ. Body Paragraph 3

A. Nature versus nurture? Which one is better

B. Nurture – environment is king

C. The environment you grow up affects you

V. Conclusion

A. Restate the thesis statement

B. Restate your arguments

C. Give one final argument

【例2】

Life in the Country

Ⅰ. Introduction

A. Background story about urban life and that in the rural area

B. Thesis Statement: I prefer life in the country to that in a city if I were to choose

Ⅱ. Life in the country

A. Good scenery and environment

B. More fun with in the trees and rivers

C. Happy with the people there

D. Quieter and more time to think over things

Ⅲ. Comparison of life in the country and that in a city

A. Stressed-out and busy with work

B. Noisy and polluted

C. No time to relax

IV. Conclusion

A. Life in the country is changing

B. Need to make money in the city

C. Still enjoying staying in the coutry now and then for a refresh and short seclusion

（三）标题—句子式混合提纲

标题—句子式混合提纲中，每个层级的内容是将若干单词、短语或者完整的句子混合使用。由于提纲撰写的目的是激发想象力从而形成思路，标题—句子混合提纲不要求在对仗整齐的问题上下太多功夫。这种形式的提纲给作者更多的灵活、自由的发挥空间，激发作者的思路如行云流水，张扬文采。混合提纲不要求形式的对称，但同一层级的内容仍然必须对等。

【例】

Life in the Country

I. Introduction

A. More and more people flee the city and choose to live in the country nowadays

1. Life in a city (noisy, busy, pressure, pollution, no time to think about things, etc.)

2. Life in the country (quiet, peaceful, clean water, clear sky, refresh, etc.)

B. Thesis Statement: It's a good idea to go to the country for a refresh and to find new inspirations in life

II. Life in the country is serene and peaceful

A. The environment (scenery, fresh air and unpolluted water, etc.)

B. More fun (walking in the tress, fishing in the rivers)

C. Quieter (more time to ponder over things, forgetting about worldly worries)

D. The people (helpful, warm, friendly, etc.)

III. Compared with life in the country, one is busy with work, stressed and with no time for a refresh

A. Stressed (work, bills to pay, dealing with people, all sorts of trivialities, etc.)

B. Environment (noisy, crowded, polluted, no good scenery, etc.)

Ⅳ. So, that's why I prefer life in the rural area to that in a city

A. Life in the country is still a good escape from the city though changes are taking place

B. Seclusion for a short while

C. Finding new inspirations and regaining new source of power for life

在上述三个提纲中，一级标题句都属于第一层级，它们都遵循了内容的对等原则，一级标题从属于主题，服务于主题，与主题具有较强的相关性，从几个侧面支撑了主题。除混合提纲外，它们的次级标题也都遵循了对等、对称的原则。

练习题

一、在下列横线中填入下列写作提纲段落中缺失部分（不需要补全完整提纲）。

1. Cheating in the Exams Should be Punished

Ⅰ. Introduction

A. Cheating never stopped appearing in all kinds of exams since a long time ago (unfair, bad for your studies, against the regulations, shame if caught, etc.)

B. Cheating in exams should be punished.

Ⅱ. Body Paragraph 1.

A. Topic Sentence:

B. The rest of the class work hard the whole semester but underestimated due to cheating (unfair, discouraging, etc.)

C. The teachers think you are doing well (missing the chancing of being corrected, dishonest, despise from other students, etc.)

D. Lose the chance of applying for scholarships (against the rules)

…

2. Away from the Takeout Food

Ⅰ. Introduction

A. More and more students buy takeouts today(delivery at door, convenient, unsafe, encourage laziness, smell terrible, cause diseases, etc.)

B. Thesis Statement: I never buy takeout foods and persuade my friends to do the same as I do.

Ⅱ. Body Paragraph 1.

A. Topic Sentence

…

Ⅲ. Body Paragraph 2.

A. Topic Sentence

…

Ⅳ. Body Paragraph 3.

A. Topic Sentence

…

V. Conclusion.

Re-state the thesis: ＿＿＿＿＿＿＿＿.

二、按要求就以下文题撰写写作提纲。

1. My Mother（a.音容笑貌；b.脾气性格；c.对家人的爱；d.对他人的善意、关心）

2. A Visit to the Great Hall of the People（参阅一下小学语文课本里原文撰写）

3. My Pet Dog（a.外表；b.聪明会算术、帮我做事；c.能陪我玩）

4. I Like Reading English Stories（a.帮助我学英语；b.知识面更广；c.了解中外风土人情；d.对课本知识的补充；e.有成就感很快乐）

5. Taking Excises Makes Me Happy（a.运动使我更健康；b.交到更多的朋友；c.使我更快乐性格更豁达；d.促进我的学习）

6. No Mobilephones in Class（a.影响自己的学习；b.影响附近的同学听课；c.影响老师情绪；d.挂科是必然的；e.结论）

三、试提取下列文章的提纲。

例如：

Essay 1

Many people value their time more than anything else in the world. Once time is gone it can never be replaced. This makes time more valuable than money.

Time is precious. Nobody can afford to waste time. Once time has gone by, it will never return. You can never turn the clock back. Time passes very quickly. People say time flies. Time and tide wait for no man. We should, therefore, make the best use of our time.

If you can manage your time well, you will have a successful life. Even a few minutes practice while waiting for the bus can be valuable learning time. Try using every bit of your spare time to practice study when it is not too late.

Example: Outline for Essay 1

Ⅰ. Introduction

A. Time is valuable.

B. Once time is gone it can never be replaced.

Ⅱ. Body

A. Time is precious.

B. Nobody can afford to waste time.

C. Once time has gone by, it will never return. You can never turn the clock back.

D. Time passes very quickly. People say time flies. Time and tide wait for no man. We should, therefore, make the best use of our time.

Ⅲ. Conclusion

A. If you can manage your time well, you will have a successful life.

B. Try using every bit of your spare time to practice study when it is not too late.

Essay 2

I study in D.A.V. Public School. There are about 35 teachers in my school, but I like my English teacher, Mrs. Sarita Sharma, very much.

She is about 30 years of age. She is of fair colour. She has been teaching in my school for the last five years.

She is a gentle lady. Her personality is very impressive. She loves me very much. She is always cheerful. She is very soft spoken.

Mrs. Sarema's motivation in teaching helped me to enjoy and do well in my class. She always teaches her students good manners and to be disciplined.

She has a keen interest in sports, too. She takes us for outdoor picnics and educational tours.

She makes her teaching interesting with the help of charts and maps. She is always ready to help her students. She is very kind to the weak and poor.

But she is very strict in discipline. Her qualities have made her the most popular teacher of my school.

Essay 3

I am a 10th class student. I attend a famous privately recognized High School. I like my life at school.

As a student, I have certain duties and responsibilities. I like them. I never try to shirk them. I take pleasure in doing what my parents bid me to do. I read and write a lot. I always try to please my teachers with my work, conduct and behaviour.

I never go against their wishes. I do my duty diligently for the sake of duty and I have nothing to fear, I know that my parents and teachers are my well-wishes. My welfare is always dear to them. They are ready to make every sacrifice for me.

Their lives are living examples for me. They set before me certain guiding principles. I follow them faithfully and have no reason to be unhappy. Nothing gives me greater pleasure than to obey my elders and do my duty honestly.

I enjoy certain rights and privileges which emanate from duty well done. The love of my parents and teachers is a rare thing for me. I feel proud of it. I get ample time to play and enjoy the company of my friends and comrades.

I am an all-round sportsman and take an active part in games like cricket, hockey, badminton and table-tennis. Games and sports help me grow up into a tall young man. They make me happy and healthy.

Scouting, hiking, mountaineering, excursions, dramas, declamations and debates make my life at school interesting and charming. I am loved and honoured by my fellow students for my achievements in studies, games and other activities.

I am free from the cares and worries of life. I am regular and methodical in my work. I work hard throughout the year. I never absent myself from school. I read new books and newspapers. I think hard. I use my head as well as my hands. I have no reason to be afraid of my teachers and examinations. My life is disciplined and well-regulated. It is all very beneficial to me.

School life is preparing me for a better and a fuller life ahead. I am preparing myself for the battle of life. The punishment for my sins of omission and commission is not painful to me. It strengthens my character and leads me on to the right path. I take great pleasure and pride in all that my school life can provide me with and stands for.

第四章　英语标点符号及空格的使用规则

标点符号是书面语中辅助文字记录语言的符号，是英语书面语的有机组成部分，它用来表示停顿、断句，表达语气、情绪、情感等。合理地使用标点符号使文章的意思更加清楚、准确，语义更加明了易懂。在有些句子中，使用不同的标点符号表达出的句子意思可能截然不同，使用不当往往会产生理解上的歧义而导致误会。英语书面语中，常见的标点符号有逗号、句号、引号、冒号、分号、省略号等。

句号 Full Stop/Period，"."

顾名思义，句号是一个句子的终结符号。当我们说完一句话时通常在句子的末尾加一个句号，有时也把它叫作句点；中文中句号是一个空心圆，英文中是一个实心点。句号写在句子末尾最后一个字母的右下方，与前面的单词间没有空格。

规则1：在完整地陈述句后用句号。

【例句】Class is over.

The plane took off.

The rain has stopped.

The peace talks ended with a cease-fire agreement.

规则2：如果句子以缩写词结尾，并且缩写词已经有一个缩写符号，此时不再使用句号。

【误】The incident happened in 456 B.C..

【正】The incident happened in 456 B.C.

规则3：如果一个句子以问号或感叹号结尾，不再用句号。

【误】Have you read the book *For Whom the Bell Tolls?*.

【正】Have you read the book *For Whom the Bell Tolls*?

【正】He used to work at Citibank!

【误】He used to work at Citibank!.

规则4：当一个句子以括号结尾时，分为两种情况：

（1）当括号中的句子属于前句的一部分时，句号放在括号外。

【例句】Hotel rooms are likely to be in short supply throughout August (the peak travel period).

（2）当括号中的内容是一个独立的句子时，句号放在括号内。

【例句】Their house was the largest one on the block. (It also happened to be the ugliest.)

规则5：如果句子以引号结束，句号置于引号内。

【例句】The president's speech both began and ended with the word "freedom."

如果引号内的内容本身以问号或感叹号结尾，句尾不需要句号。

【正】Laura said, "We will continue this tomorrow at 8:00 a.m."

【误】Laura said, "We will continue this tomorrow at 8:00 a.m." .

【正】Yesterday he asked, "Why is it so cold on Mars?"

【误】Yesterday he asked, "Why is it so cold on Mars?" .

逗号 Comma，","

逗号和句号是英语中使用频率最高的两个标点符号，也是使用错误最多的。如果说句号表示一个句子终了的话，逗号表示句子中间的停顿。

规则1：逗号将并列的两个或两个以上的词隔开。这个用法相当于中文中的顿号（英语中没有顿号）。

【例句】We visited Britain, France, Italy and Germany.

At school, we study Chinese, math, physics, chemistry, etc.

有时，为了避免造成误解，and/or 之前也需要添加一个逗号，请看下句。

【例句】We had coffee, cheese and crackers and grapes.

本句中，由于 cheese and crackers是一种点心，应该在crackers之后添加一个逗号明确表示出来。

【修改后】We had coffee, cheese and crackers, and grapes.

规则2：用逗号来分隔两个或两个以上的形容词，一般用于两个可以互换位置的形容词。

【正】She is a pretty, warm-hearted girl.

本句中两个形容词是可以互相交换位置的，如我们也可以说：

【正】She is a warm-hearted，pretty girl.

有些情况下形容词的位置不能互换。例如：

【正】We stayed at an expensive summer resort.

因此，本例中我们不能说：

【误】We stayed at a summer, expensive resort.

要判断两个形容词之间是不是需要一个逗号，可以尝试在两个形容词之间添加一个and，如果添加后句子还能成立，就可以加逗号；如果添加and后句子不通顺，就不能添加逗号。

上面的例子中，a pretty and warm-hearted girl是通顺的，而an expensive and summer resort 是不能成立的，所以在expesive和summer之间不能有逗号。

规则3：两个独立成句的句子中间不能使用逗号而应该使用句号，否则将导致几个句子混淆在一起，每句话的意思都说不清，在写作实践中这种错误叫万能逗号，也有人把它翻译成逗号粘连。

【误】She went abroad, she sold the house.

以上错误可以有如下多种纠正办法：

【正】She went abroad. She sold the house.

【正】She sold the house before she went abroad.

【正】She went abroad, and she sold the house.

规则4：如果两个独立的句子由and, or, but, such等连接词连接，在第一个句子后添加逗号。

【误】She went abroad and she sold the house.

【正】She went abroad, and she sold the house.

在短句子中逗号可以省略。例如：

【正】I paint and he writes.

现代英语中，由于很多作者不懂或者不屑于这条规则，所以在很多长句子中在and前不加逗号。由于语言是社会性的，它具有从众的属性，说的人多了便也就对了。文字是记录作为某个群体全体成员所共同接受并通用的口头语言的一套符号系统，大家都这么用它就是对的，标点符号作为文字的一部分也不例外。

规则5：一个句子中如果有两个谓语动词，且都是由同一个主语执行，则句中不需要添加逗号。

【例句】She worked hard but still failed the exam.

如果一个句子中有两个谓语动词，并且分别由两个主语执行，则需要用一个逗号隔开。

【误】I saw that she was busy and prepared to leave.

【正】I saw that she was busy, and prepared to leave.

上例中，如果不添加逗号，读者很可能会理解为"she"准备离开，而实际上要离开的是"I"。

规则6：在复合句中，如果从句在前、主句在后，则需要在从句前置一逗号。反之如果主句在前、从句在后，则无须逗号。此类句子中的连接词通常有if, because, whole, as, although, since, unless等。

【正】If any changes have been made to the schedule, let me know now.

【正】Please let me know if any changes have been made to the schedule.

【正】We were late for class because it rained hard.

【正】Because it rained hard, so we were late for class.

规则7：单词、短语及其他独立结构等非关键信息需要用逗号与句中主要信息隔开。尤其当这些非关键信息出现在句子中间时逗号的作用尤为重要，需要前后用逗号与主要信息隔开。

【误】Jill who is my sister shut the door.

【正】Jill, who is my sister, shut the door.

【误】The man knowing it was late hurried home.

【正】The man, knowing it was late, hurried home.

同位语也需要用逗号隔开。

【误】Her best friend, Amy arrived.

【正】Her best friend, Amy, arrived.

【误】The three items, a book, a pen, and paper were on the table.

【正】The three items, a book, a pen, and paper, were on the table.

规则8：如果某人或某物前文已经提到过或者听众及读者都知道其所指，则在句中是非关键性信息，后面的定语从句或限定性短语需要用逗号隔开。

【例句】Jane, who appeared on TV for Super Girl Contest, came to our community yesterday.

本例中，听话者都知道是哪一个Jane，所以who appeared on TV for Super Girl Contest为非关键性信息，须置一逗号隔开。

如果我们不知道指的是哪一位Jane，需要补充信息加以说明，这种情况不可添加逗号。

【例句】Jane who appeared on TV for Super Girl Contest came to our community yesterday.

规则9：插入语或句中的独立结构须前后都使用一个逗号隔开。

【例句】He, on behalf of the whole class, spoke at the meeting.

规则10：句中如果含有人的名字、称呼或昵称需要用逗号前后隔开。

【例句】Could he, old Jack, still recognize me?

Yes, Mum, I will.

God bless you, my dear son.

规则11：在表示日期时，用来分隔年份和月份。

【例句】She was born on the February 8, 2001.

在使用这条规则时，需要注意的是无论顺序如何，月份和日期中间都不使用逗号。

【正】The incident took place on September 6.

【正】The incident took place on 6 September.

规则12：用在地名中，遵循小地点在前大地点在后的原则，且中间置一逗号隔开。

【例句】He lives in Haikou City, Hainan Province, the People's Republic of China.

规则13：直接引语前用逗号。

【例句】She said, "I can't hear you clearly."

"Now," I asked, "can you hear me clearly?"

如果句子很短也可忽略本条规则。

【例句】He said "Stop."

规则14：如果直接引语出现在诸如he said, she wrote, they reported, Mary insisted之前，直接引语的引号内无论句子长短都用逗号结尾。应该强调的是，此种情形下即使原直接引语以句号结尾此时引号内也用逗号。

【例句】"That hardly ever happened around here," he said.

"Stop," he said.

规则15：表示等等的etc.前通常应该添加一个逗号。

【例句】Sleeping bags, pans, warm clothing, etc., are in the tent.

问号 Question Mark，"？"

一般疑问句或特殊疑问句结尾用问号。此外，直接引语中的问句结尾用问号，间接引语中原句的问号需要改成句号。例如：

【直接引语】I asked, "Where did you go?"

【间接引语】I wondered where she went.

感叹号（Exclamation Point/mark，"！"）

感叹号用来表达较为强烈的感情，如惊讶、恐惧、愤怒等。

规则1：感叹号通常用于表达感情、强调或惊讶。

【例句】I'm truly shocked by your behavior!

Yay! We won!

规则2：句中、句尾出现了感叹号，则不再重复使用句号或逗号。

【正】I'm truly shocked by your behavior!

【误】I'm truly shocked by your behavior!

【正】"I'm truly shocked by your behavior!" I told her.

【误】"I'm truly shocked by your behavior!", I told her.

【正】"Get out!" Marcus yelled.

【误】"Get out!", Marcus yelled.

规则3：感叹号有较浓厚的个人感情色彩，为了显得正式庄重，正式文件及商务信函通常不使用感叹号。其他文体写作中除非有较为强烈的感情需要表达，也应该尽量避免使用感叹号。

分号 Semicolon，";"

分号用来分隔两个相对独立又有一定关系的句子，且当在这两个独立成句的句子之间没有连接词（for, and, or, but, yet, so, etc.）。分号语气比逗号强、比句号弱，因此朗读时的停顿比逗号稍长比句号稍短。

规则1：如果两个独立的句子在句意上有一定的联系，使用分号，不用句号，并且第二个句子首字母通常不大写。

【例句】He went out of the room; he locked the door.

We have paid our dues; we expect all the privileges listed in the contract.

规则2：句中若出现一个主句和一个从句，则构成一个复合句。当从句在前、主句在后时，要使用逗号，不能用分号。

【误】Although she got up earlier than usual; she was late for work.

【正】Although she got up earlier than usual, she was late for work.

规则3：在namely, however, therefore, that is, i.e., for example, e.g., for instance等连接词前使用分号。通常情况下，需在这些连接词后加一个逗号。

【例句】

Bring any two items; however, sleeping bags and tents are in short supply.

He left here last night; namely, he is not here now.

There are several functions for a smartphone; for example, making a phone call, chatting with your friends or searching the internet.

规则4：用来分隔并列的几个词组，且当词组本身含有逗号。

【误】The athletes come from Beijing, China, California, USA, London, UK, Paris, France, etc.

上例中，没有分号的分隔作用，对句子的理解会造成极大的困难。

【正】The athletes come from Beijing, China; California, USA; London, UK; Paris, France, etc.

规则5：在并列的从句之间，如果前面的从句中已经包含逗号，即使后面的从句有and, but, or, nor等连接词引导，两句也应该用分号隔开。

【例句】When I finish here, and I will soon, I'll be glad to help you; and that is a promise I will keep.

规则6：分号后面的句子首字母不大写。

【误】I am here; You are over there.

【正】I am here; you are over there.

冒号 Colon，":"

冒号，意为"亦即；就是说"，表示后面还有对前述内容的具体说明。

规则1：用来导出后面的具体内容，首字母不大写。

【例句】

You know what to do: practice.

You may be required to bring many things: sleeping bags, pans, utensils, and warm clothing.

I want the following items: butter, sugar, and flour.

I need an assistant who can do the following: input data, write reports, and complete tax forms.

He got what he worked for: a promotion

He got what he worked for: a promotion that paid a higher wage.

规则2：如果导出的具体内容与主句的动词有动宾关系，不可使用冒号。

【不妥】I want: butter, sugar, and flour.

【正确】I want butter, sugar, and flour.

但是，下面的说法是正确的：

【正】Here is what I want: butter, sugar, and flour.

规则3：如果冒号后是一个一连串句子，每句独立成句，并且每句各占一行，则首字母需要大写，句尾需要句号。如果冒号下面是一系列的单词或词组，并且各占一行，可不用任何标点符号。下列例句不需要大写与句号。

【例句】

I want an assistant who can do the following:

input data

write reports

complete tax forms

下列例句首字母需要大写，句尾需要句号。

【例句】

The following are requested:

Wool sweaters for possible cold weather.

Wet suits for snorkeling.

Introductions to the local dignitaries.

【例句】

These are the swimming-pool rules:

Do not run.

If you see unsafe behavior, report it to the lifeguard.

Did you remember your towel?

Have fun!

规则4：两个独立的句子，如果后句为前句起着解释、说明或者补充等作用，则两句中间可添加一个冒号。

【例句】He got what he worked for: He really earned that promotion.

Remember the old saying: Be careful what you wish for.

规则5：冒号后跟直接引语时，引号内的句子首字母要大写。

【例句】The host made an announcement: "You are all staying for dinner."

规则6：商务信函中，称呼之后用通常用冒号，非正式文体中称呼后一般用逗号。

【例句】

Dear Mr. Smith:

Dear Dave,

引号 Quotation Marks，双引号""/单引号''

直接引语需要放在引号中。引号分单引号（single quotation mark）和双引号（double quotation mark），其中单引号只用在一个直接引语中所含有的另一个直接引语里。

规则1：直接引用其他作品中的文字，需要置于引号中。

【正】"I hope you will be here," he said.

【误】He said that he "hoped I would be there."（*hoped I would be there*不是原话，应为间接引语。）

规则2：不管直接引语处于句中什么位置，只要是完整的句子引号中的句子首字母总是要大写。而且，如果he said等词语出现在直接引语之前，引号前需要置一逗号或冒号。

【例句】He said, "The case is far from over, and we will win."

规则3：如果引用的不是完整的句子，而是成为本句的一部分时，首字母不需要大写。

【例句】He said that the case was "far from over" and that "we will win".

规则4：如果直接引语出现在he said, she wrote, they reported等之前，则直接引语以逗号结尾。

【例句】"I don't care," he said.

"Stop," he said.

规则5：如果直接引语在句中作主语或宾语等成分时，则直接引语的结尾不需要标点符号。

【例句】Is "I don't care" all you can say to me?

Saying "Stop the car" was a mistake.

规则6：句号和逗号总是放在引号内。

【例句】The sign said, "Walk." Then it said, "Don't Walk," then, "Walk," all within thirty seconds.

He yelled, "Hurry up."

规则7：问号放在引号内还是引号外视情况而定。如果原句中带有问号，则问号置于引号内，否则通常置于引号外。

【例句】She asked, "Will you still be my friend?"

The question "Will you still be my friend?" is part of the quotation.

Do you agree with the saying, "All's fair in love and war"?

The question "Do you agree with the saying?" is outside the quotation.

规则8：如果直接引语出现在句子前端，并且是一个问句，则问号后不再重复使用逗号，这也是标点符号不得重复使用原则。

【例句】"Will you still be my friend?" she asked.

规则9：如果直接引语中还有直接引语，通常里面的那个直接引语要使用单引号，这是唯一需要使用单引号的场合。如果单引号与双引号相遇，则留一定间距。

【例句】Dan said: "In a town outside Brisbane, I saw 'Tourists go home' written on a wall. But then someone told me, 'Pay it no mind, lad.' "

规则10：如果引用的直接引语不止一段，则每段开始处使用一个引号，但结尾处不需要引号，最后一段直接引语处添加一个引号收尾即可。

【例句】She wrote: "I don't paint anymore. For a while I thought it was just a phase that I'd get over.

Now, I don't even try."

括号 Parentheses and brackets

与中文里一样，英语里括号有小括号"( )"、中括号"[]"、大括号"{}"（braces）和尖括号（angle brackets）等几种。我们只介绍其中的小括号和中括号。其中parentheses 是小括号又叫圆括号；brackets是中括号，中文里又叫方括号。

A. 小括号 Parentheses"( )"

小括号内的内容用来对前述内容加以说明与补充。

【例句】He finally answered (after taking five minutes to think) that he did not understand the question.

规则1：如果括号内的内容出现在句尾，句号置于括号的外面。

【例句】He gave me a nice bonus ($500).

规则2：如果括号内是一个完整的句子，则括号内的句子结尾处需要一个相应的标点符号。

【例句】Please read the analysis. (You'll be amazed.)

You are late (aren't you?).

You heard what I said. (Didn't you?)

规则3：括号前通常不可使用逗号，括号后需要时可以添加逗号。

【误】When he got home, (it was already dark outside) he cooked dinner.

【正】When he got home (it was already dark outside), he cooked dinner.

B. 中括号 Brackets"[ ]"

中文里，中括号又叫方括号，它的使用范围远不及小括号广，通常只用于对引用的文献加以说明。

规则1：中括号内放置作者、译者或编者对其引用文献的说明或解释。

【例句】"Four score and seven [today we'd say eighty-seven] years ago..."

"Bill shook hands with [his son] Al."

规则2：在论文写作中，当引用的文献中存在错误或疑似不当之处，作者或译者需要说明时，将说明内容放置在中括号内，前面写上斜体的拉丁缩写词*sic.* 纠正正文不需要斜体。其中, sic 意为"原文如此。"

【例句】She wrote, "I would rather die then [sic] be seen wearing the same outfit as my sister." [sic]表示原文中then为than的误用。

规则3：本条规则在论文写作中也非常有用。在正式的文体中，使用中括号既能保留被引用原文的原貌，同时又能兼顾本句的得体性。

【例句】"[T]he better angels of our nature" gave a powerful ending to Lincoln's first inaugural address.

本例中，原文为首字母为小写，被引用后放置在句首，需要改为大写，所以需要用中括号注明。

撇号 Apostrophe，" ' "

撇号常用来表示单词的缩写及名词的所有格，同时在某些特定的时候还能表达复数。

规则1：表示缩写。缩写在英语写作中广泛使用，但是正式文体中要尽量避免使用缩写形式。

【例句】It's often said that every dog has its day.

Let's not forget that grandma lets the kids eat way too much junk food when they stay with her.

规则2：年份的省略方式表达。

【例如】the class of '85(1985)

pop music from the '80s(nineteen eighties)

但是，完整的年份的复数形式不能用此方法表达。请注意以下的例子。

【正】Since the 1980s, the Thomases, both of whom have multiple PhDs, have sold old books and magazines at the fair on Saturdays and Sundays.

【误】Since the 1980's, the Thomas's, both of whom have multiple PhD's, have sold old book's and magazine's at the fair on Saturday's and Sunday's.

规则3：特殊情况下撇号可以表达复数，即少数缩写形式、字母或者单词的复数形式需要使用撇号。

【例句】He received four A's and two B's.

We hired three M.D.'s and two D.O.'s.

Be sure to cross your t's and dot your i's.

Do we have more yes's than no's?

但是有些情况下不可使用"撇号+s"来构成名词的复数形式。

【误】Apostrophe's are confusing.

【正】Apostrophes are confusing.

【误】We've had many happy Christmas's.

【正】We've had many happy Christmases.

少数特殊情况下，由于上下文的需要将一些其他词性用成名词复数形式时，为了避免造成混淆，可以在s前添加撇号。

【例句】Here are some do's and don'ts.

You are always depending of if's.

当某些缩写词、字母（尤其是小写字母）等用作复数时，需要添加撇号。但是，只要不会造成理解错误尽量不要使用撇号。

【例句】My a's look like u's.

There are two s's and m's in this word.

He received four A's and two B's.

We hired three M.D.'s and two D.O.'s.

Be sure to cross your t's and dot your i's.

Do we have more yes's than no's?

There are two l's in the word.

Please find letter A's in the whole line.

有时候，两个以上的大写字母的缩写词的复数，可不添加撇号。本规则中如果大写字母的缩写词以缩写符号点结束则一般需要一个撇号。

【例句】There are two new MPs on the base.

He learned his ABCs.

She consulted with three M.D.s. OR She consulted with three M.D.'s.

Some write M.D.'s to give the s separation from the second period.

规则4：表达单数名词的所有格。

【例如】a woman's hat

Mrs. Zhang's house

the boss's wife

（1）在复数名词后或者以s结尾的名词后，只用撇号，不再添加s。本规则在理论界具有争议性，但我国主流英语教材中普遍采用本条规则。

【例如】the class' hours

Mr. Jones' golf clubs

the canvas's size

Texas' weather

Mr. Hastings' pen

在使用此条规则时需要注意的是，有些英语姓氏本身以s结尾，表达"一家人"这个概念时需要先添加es，然后再使用撇号。

【误】the Hastings' dog

【正】the Hastingses' dog (Hastings + es + apostrophe)

【误】the Jones' car

【正】the Joneses' car

此外，名词的规则变化形式通常在单词末尾添加s或es。如果要表达所有格，仅添加一个撇号。

【正】guys' night out (guy + s + apostrophe)

【误】guy's night out (implies only one guy)

【正】two actresses' roles (actress + es + apostrophe)

【误】two actress's roles

（2）表示某人对某物的拥有。

A. 如果表示两人的共同用有，只在第二个名词后添加撇号。此种用法中，如果其中一方是物主代词，应该使用形容词性的物主代词。

【正】Jane and Kate's room

【误】Maribel and my home

【误】Mine and Maribel's home

【正】Maribel's and my home

【误】he and Maribel's home

【误】him and Maribel's home

【正】his and Maribel's home

【误】you and Maribel's home

【误】yours and Maribel's home

【正】Maribel's and your home

B. 如果并非两人共有，而是分别拥有，则需要分别添加一个"撇号+s"构成所有格。

【例句】

Cesar's and Maribel's homes are both lovely.（各自拥有）

Cesar and Maribel's home is lovely.（共同拥有）

（3）时间与金钱单位的复数用作定语时通常需要一个撇号。

【误】three days leave

【正】three days' leave

【误】my two cents worth

【正】my two cents' worth

连字符 Hyphen，"–"

连字符的主要功能是把两个或两个以上的单词连接起来，以形成一个新的复合名词或复合形容词。连字符还可以在排版时用来表示移行。

复合词指由两个或两个以上的词合成的词，合成后的词形成一个新词，具有新的意思。约定俗成的复合词经过长期使用已经被普遍接受，则可不用连字符。复合词通常有三种存在形式，即开放式、闭合式和连接式。

【开放式】printing press

car wash

chief of staff

【连接式】eye-opener

check-in

free-for-all

【闭合式】bookstore

whodunit

规则1：用于形成复合形容词，通常放置于被修饰词的前面作定语。

【例如】an off-campus apartment

state-of-the-art design

a seven-day holiday

an nine-inch television

a 100-meter building

a five-year-old boy

通常情况下，如果在句中作表语不需要添加连字符，但有些约定俗成的复合词已经被广为接受，连字符需要保留。

【例句】The apartment is off campus.

The design is state-of-the-art.

规则2：有时在写作中出于幽默、讽刺、烘托气氛或特殊情境描写的需要，建议使用连字符。这种用法经常出现在小说、新闻报道或小品文中。

【例句】The slacker video-gamed his way through life.

Queen Victoria throne-sat for six decades.

规则3：自己造的词必须用连字符连接起来，避免引起误会。

【例句】There was a hit-and-run accident yesterday.

He came from an out-of-the-way village.

Give-and-take principles prevail in this area.

They played hide-and-seek.

It was a risk-life, pleasure-seeking sport.

规则4：用于时间跨度、距离或范围等数量单位中。在这种情形中，有些人使用比连字符稍长一点的en dash（连接号）。为了避免麻烦，在我国的英语教科书中不提倡使用连接号，我们也不对此专门加以介绍。

【例如】3:15–3:45 p.m.

1999–2016

300–325 people

【En Dashes】3:15–3:45 p.m.

1999–2016

300–325 people

数字twenty-one到ninety-nine都需要用连字符连接。

【例如】thirty-two children

one thousand two hundred twenty-one dollars

规则5：分子与分母之间需要用连字符连接，但如果分子前面有a或者an时则无需连接。

【例句】More than one-third of registered voters oppose the measure.

More than a third of registered voters oppose the measure.

类似于分数的用法还有下面的例子。

【正】The sign is five and one-half feet long.

【正】A five-and-one-half-foot-long sign.

【误】The sign is five-and-one-half feet long.

规则6：专有名词作定语时不可使用连字符。

【误】She is an Academy-Award nominee.

【正】She is an Academy Award nominee.

规则7：外国人名的双姓氏通常要用连字符连接在一起。

【例句】Sir Winthrop Heinz-Eakins will attend the meeting.

规则8：表达祖先时，great后需要使用连字符，grand后不需要因为grandfather/grandmother已经形成一个单词。

【例句】My grandson and my granduncle never met.

My great-great-grandfather fought in the Civil War.

总体上说，加不加连字符以权威性的词典为准。即使不会引起误会有些作者在所有的复合词间均添加连字符，以示严谨，这样做也无可厚非。

规则9：前缀及后缀的连字符使用规则。

英语中另外一经常使用到连字符的地方就是前缀（prefix）和后缀（suffix)。

（1）专有名词前要使用连字符。

【例如】trans-American

mid-July

mid-Autumn Day

（2）很多时候，当词根首字母与前缀尾字母是同一个元音字母的时候，需要加连字符。

【例如】ultra-ambitious

semi-invalid

re-elect

（3）以self-, ex-以及all-开头的词，原则上均需要添加连字符。

【例如】self-assured

ex-mayor

all-knowing

all-round

（4）为了避免引起误解，有些地方必须使用连字符，如前缀re-。

【例句】Will she recover from her illness?

I have re-covered the sofa twice.

上例中第一句本身就是一个单词意为恢复的意思，而第二句如果不使用连字符，读者很难读懂本句想说什么。

【例句】I must re-press the shirt.

上面的句子中，如果没有连字符，读者很可能会把re-press（重新按压即熨烫）理解成repress（镇压）。

（5）如果没有连字符会造成语义含糊不清，则添加连字符。

【例如】de-ice

co-worker

上面的例子中，de-ice与deice是两个不同的单词；在第二个例子中，不加连字符，容易使读者把第一个音节误以为是cow。

规则10：固定搭配中的后缀通常已经长期存在，已经形成一个单独的单词，除极个别单词外不需要添加连字符。

【例如】scientist

Marxism

racism

edible

impossible

（1）通常情况下后缀是已经形成单词被人们广泛接受，但-style, -elect, -free,-base等例外。

【例如】Modernist-style paintings

president-elect

sugar-free soda

oil-based sludge

（2）如果后缀的首字母与词根的最后一个字母相同，则需要加一个连字符。

【例如】graffiti-ism

wiretap-proof

总之，一个复合词中是不是需要用连字符，如果不能确定，就需要查阅权威词典或者上网查一下。虽然花点时间，但是比用错了好。

破折号 Em Dash，"—"

破折号通常用来对前述内容加以说明、补充、强调或证明等。本节中提到的破折号英文名称叫am dash，英语中还有连接符（en dash），它与破折号是不同的，连接符在前节中已经提及这里不再赘述。值得注意的是，目前出版物中破折号都叫dash，对em dash/en dash不做无意义的区分。

注意以下句子里在添加了破折号以后语气上的不同。

【例句】

You are the friend, the only friend, who offered to help me.（表示说话者有不止一个朋友，只有句中提到的朋友帮助了"我"。）

You are the friend—the only friend—who offered to help me.（表示说话者"我"只有一个朋友，这唯一的一个朋友帮助了"我"。）

I pay the bills; she has all the fun.（表示她一直在玩。）

I pay the bills—she has all the fun.（强调她只知道玩。）

规则1：独立于主题之外的内容通常需要用破折号隔开。

【例句】Joe—and his trusty mutt—was always welcome.

规则2：破折号与逗号不重复使用。

【无破折号】The man from London, UK, arrived.

【有破折号】The man—from London, UK—arrived.

省略号Ellipses, "..."

省略号由三个句点组成。当我们在引用别人的内容且需要省略某些词的时候，就可以使用省略号来表明。省略号的功能是将不想要的或者不相关的内容从引用的文字中省略掉，以达到直奔主题的效果。省略号前后的一个字母的间隙，可以留也可以不留。

【例句】

"Today, after hours of careful thought, we vetoed the bill."（全文引用）

"Today … we vetoed the bill."（省略引用）

省略号可用来表达犹豫不决、思绪飘忽不定等情绪上的变化。

【例句】

I don't know … I'm not sure.

Pride is one thing, but what happens if she …

He said, "I … really don't … understand this."

此外，用三个点 "..." 表示省略了一些字，用四个点 "...." 则表示省略了一些句子。

第五章　英语写作中的移行规则

在英语写作中有时候会涉及移行（division of words at the end of a line），移行的目的是使文章的右边界看上去整齐一些。移行时连字符置于上一行的末尾以表明该单词后半部分已经移往下一行。

移行首先要考虑的是如何合理地拆分单词，而单词的拆分是要遵循一定规则的。如果随意地对单词进行拆分，会增加读者对单词词义理解的难度、难以判断其正确发音，更有甚者会引起读者对词义的误解。所以，不到万不得已尽量不要移行。移行时通常要保证读者在看到上一行中单词的前半部分就能判断出其读音或者语义，结合下一行的后半部分就能基本判断出本单词的完整词义或读音。如果不能做到这一点，建议不要轻易地进行移行操作。

英语单词的音节划分是有一些现成的规则的，学习这些规则之后基本上能够掌握正确移行的方法。移行时，仅仅了解音节的划分是不够的。对于确实无法正确划分音节的单词，可以查询比较权威的词典；目前在线词典基本上都对单词的音节进行标注。在对英语单词进行移行时，还要保证不影响读者对其语义及读音的判断，所以移行时往往不能仅仅根据音节的划分来决定哪些音节留在上一行、哪些音节移到下一行，还要考虑单词的词源、词根、前缀、后缀及读音规则等因素，如果是复合词也要保证构成该词两个部分的完整性，以免造成歧义，给读者的阅读带来理解上的困难或错误的联想。例如：

【正】co-inci-dencere-appear

【误】coin-cidencereap-pear

上例中，如果coincidence拆分成coin-cidence而不是co-inci-dence，将会引起读者错误的联想，给阅读带来麻烦。

大部分英语单词的音节都是按读音来划分的，如a-fraid, be-tween, lov-er,

cov-er, clo-ver, i-de-a, id-i-om, ra-di-a-tor, rad-i-cal, po-ta-to, pop-u-lar, com-pat-i-ble, crim-i-nal, ta-ble。英语单词在划分音节的时候要考虑重读、弱读、长元音及短元音等因素，如fin-ish, fi-nal; fin-ger, sing-er; riv-er, fla-vor; fa-ther, moth-er; forc-ing, for-ci-ble; re-sist-i-ble, re-sis-tive; re-spon-si-ble, re-spon-sive; vis-i-ble, vi-sion; op-por-tu-ni-ty, ca-pac-i-ty, cit-y.

有相当一部分的单词是根据其构成成分来划分音节的，如前缀、后缀、词根等；在具体划分时不要割裂其完整的自然读音，如friend-ship, de-part-ment, dis-turb-ance, use-less-ness, for-get-ful, ac-count-a-ble, mis-lead-ing, aw-ful-ly, con-se-quent-ly。

当然，音节划分规律不是万能的移行规则，音节的起始点也不一定就是拆分单词的合适节点，没有把握正确划分的时候一定要查词典。最好的办法还是不拆分、不移行。如果确实需要移行，切记要保证不影响对单词的判断理解及正确读音为最高原则。下面介绍英语写作中较为常见的移行规则。

通常情况下，标题不要移行。一个段落中最后一个单词也不宜移行。换页时也不可移行，同一页中移行也不可太频繁，以两到三次为宜。

缩略词、缩写词、电子信箱、网址、电话号码、数字等都不要移行。专有名词如地名、人名也不可拆开进行移行，太短的单词也不可移行。数字、日期尽量不要移行。

移行时，需要在上一行末尾添加一个连字符。如果连字符已经存在，如复合词中，则在原有连字符后换行不另行添加连字符。例如，anti-inflationary, pre-Christian, self-confident, twenty-seven。

规则1：单音节单词不要移行，包括过去式形式-ed也不可拆分进行移行，如course, source, cause, through, draught, bought, liked, burned, played, tired, mowed, drowned, grouped, stopped, watched, laughed.

规则2：以一个字母形式存在的音节，不可将一个字母留在上一行的行末，或下一行的行首，如a-bout, a-long, a-way, a-bridged, e-lect, e-nough, snow-y, hair-y, wear-y, pneumoni-a, a-polog-y。

规则3：缩写词、缩略词或者数字不要移行。

规则4：太短的单词不建议移行。移行时通常上一行及下一行各保留至少三个字母，满足不了这个条件的尽量不移行。两个音节的单词一般不移行。例如，kitchen, hobby, worker, answer, flower, retell, receive, account, affirm, inquire, belong, because, between, invite, include, painted, crowded, catches; easily, informer, video, radio, radial, menial。

规则5：双元音或某些长元音不移行，尤其是当某些字母组合表示的是一个长元音/双元音的时候不可拆分。例如，clown, count, plough, though, load, pain, height; broom, heart, broad。

规则6：固定的辅音连缀不可割裂、移行。某些辅音连缀对应的是某一个辅音，不可随意拆分，导致无法拼读。例如，ch, tch, dge, sh, th, ck, gh, ph, ng, gu, qu, que。我们在对这种单词划分音节时必须保留辅音连缀的完整性，如match-ing, knowledge-able, breath-ing, pack-age, laugh-ter, daugh-ter, trium-phant, hang-ing, sing-ing, lin-guist, lin-guis-tics, lan-guage等。

规则7：前缀与词根之间、词根与后缀之间可以移行，前提是拆分后每部分都有三个以上的字母。例如，com-bine, argu-ment, cour-age, law-yer, play-ful, con-sist-ing, over-whelm-ing, fan-tas-tic, pre-dict-able, for-give-ness, dis-trust-ful-ness, dis-turb-ance, mis-under-stand-ing, over-estima-tion, com-mit-ment, sub-mis-sive, super-intend-ency。

规则8：如果一个单词可以有多种拆分方法，目前通行的做法是将词根和后缀分开再换行。例如，unpredict-able, respect-ful, educa-tional, revolu-tionary, deliver-ance, depart-ment, memoriza-tion, experi-ence, signa-ture, unselfish-ness。

规则9：自成一个音节的元音字母，可以在其后面移行，如crimi-nal, criti-cism, prepara-tory, litera-ture, irrele-vant, signifi-cance, opportu-nity, popu-lar, popula-tion, experi-ment, experi-ence, resi-dence, coinci-dence。

如果单词中有两个元音字母，划分音节时分为两种情况：（1）如果该辅音前面的元音为短元音时，辅音归属于上一音节；（2）如果该辅音前面的元音是发长音或者是双元音时，该辅音字母划入下一音节并移到下一行。

【辅音字母前元音发短音】

unlim-ited, pov-erty, mod-ern

【辅音字母前元音发长音】

rea-son, poi-son, fla-vor, pow-der, thou-sand

规则10：在两个自成一个音节的字母中间移行，如gradu-ation, humili-ation。中国学生习惯了汉语拼音中声母韵母的拼读方法，对这种音节划分可能很陌生，两个发短音的元音划分音节时，可以查一下词典，按照上面标的做就行。具体可以参看上一条规则。

规则11：双写的辅音字母可以拆分。例如，hap-piness, ban-ner, god-dess, lit-tle, puz-zle, car-riage, hap-pen, suf-fix, get-ting, mis-sion, mes-sage, pas-sen-ger, excel-lent, incor-rect, bal-loon, hor-rible, mil-len-nium。例外的词如pass-er的音节划分，要根据词根和后缀的规则，否则将影响理解。

规则12：分属前后两个音节的相邻的两个辅音字母可以拆分。例如，bor-der, lin-ger, mas-ter, blis-ter, fil-ter, bur-den, car-pet, ban-quet, wor-ship, cor-vette, recog-nize, expen-sive, collec-tive, respec-tive。

规则13：一个单词中有三个辅音字母相邻，如果第一个辅音前的元音为短音（参见音节划分一节），则在第一个辅音后对单词进行拆分。例如，chil-dren, coun-try, hun-gry, mon-grel, han-dle, han-dler, scram-ble, scram-bler, mon-ster, mon-strous, demon-strate, frus-trate, child-less, hand-some, monk-hood, punc-ture。

规则14：现在分词、动名词中的ing移到下一行。例如，read-ing, writ-ing, divid-ing, deny-ing, judg-ing, manag-ing, notic-ing, forc-ing, turn-ing, hurt-ing, hold-ing, find-ing。但是，如果ing前还有一个双写的辅音字母，则其中一个一同移到下一行：split-ting, swim-ming, refer-ring。这条规则例外的单词有spell-ing, call-ing, process-ing。

规则15：以ling结尾的单词，如果是名词（而不是动词+ing的变形形式），移行时ling通常移到下一行。例如，dar-ling, duck-ling。

但是，动名词或现在分词（即动词+ling后的变化形式），要遵循该动词原形的音节划分优先的原则，如nes-tling（nes-tle的动名词或现在分词），han-dling, bus-tling, scram-bling, stum-bling,dwindling。

规则16：某些后缀在移行时要整体移到下一行，不能拆分，如tion, sion, cion, gion, cial, sial, tial, cious, geous, tious, able, ible. 类似的词有：condi-tion, selec-tion, exten-sion, discus-sion, suspi-cion, reli-gion, spe-cial, commer-cial, essen-tial, deli-cious, subcon-scious, gor-geous, ambi-tious, cau-tious, reli-able, accept-able, manage-able, incred-ible, resist-ible, respon-sible, incorri-gible。

规则17：复合词的拆分原则是保留构成该词的两部分的完整性，如court-martial, 而不能划分为court-mar-tial。有连字符的复合词原连字符放在上一行，不再另行添加。

【无连字符的复合词】class-room, basket-ball, play-ground, auto-mobile, after-noon, ball-room, photo-graph, tele-vision, psycho-therapy

【本身有连字符的复合词】dining-hall, attorney-general, great-grandfather, self-confident, nineteen-eighties

规则18：移行时，下半部分不可移到下一页，即每页的最后一个单词不移行。同时无论在任何地方，一段的最后一行中最后一个单词建议不进行移行操作。

规则19：有可能会引起读者错误联想的情况不要拆分、移行，如read-just, reap-pear, wo-men, coin-cidence , sour-ces。

规则20：下半部分无法按照读音规则读出的，不要拆分、移行。

【误】probab-le broug-ht

【正】prob-able brou-ght

第六章 英语句子常见语病及修改

由于各种各样的原因，句子中难免会出现语病。语病在初学者学习过程中长期存在，有些错误在以英语为母语的国家的语言教学中也不鲜见。常见的语病具有普遍性，探讨常见错误（common errors）可以提前了解这些错误并预防它们的发生。英语中常见的语病包括无标点句（fused sentences)、万能逗号（comma splice)、定语垂悬（dangling and misplaced Modifiers)、句子成分残缺（sentence fragment）、平行结构（parallelism）以及语句不简练（wordiness and redundancy）等。下面分别进行介绍。

第一节 无标点句

两个或两个以上独立的句子之间没有标点符号断句在英语里叫fused sentence，有些地方把它翻译成"熔句"，但是"熔句"不能反映出其真实含义，这里不予采用。两个独立的句子之间没有标点符号，也就是句子融到一起了。我们形象地把它翻译成无标点句，方便理解、记忆。

所谓的无标点句，有时也指两个或两个以上独立的句子之间既没有任何标点符号也没有连接词予以连接，造成两个或多个句子堆砌在一起的现象。这种句子解决方法有两个：

（1）添加适当的标点符号，如逗号、分号或句号。

（2）添加适当的连接词，如and/ or/but/either…or/neither…nor, etc. 例如：

【误】

1. I got up washed my faced ate my breakfast went to the classroom.

2. She did some online shopping read a few pages of the book fed her cat made a phone call to her friend.

3. The dog barked she began to run she fell over a stone she broke her head she cried.

无标点句子通常发生在初学者的习作中。无标点句的修改通常是添加正确的标点符号和正确的连接词。解决办法有如下几种。

（1）在句子之间添加逗号，并用合适的连接词连接，如and, or, but, for, nor, so, yet。

（2）两个句子之间使用分号。

（3）两个句子之间使用句号。

（4）使用连接词将两个句子变成主句与从句的关系，常用的连接词有after, although, because, before, if, since, though, unless, until, when, where, and while。

（5）重写该句子。

基于以上的原则上面的无标点句可以做如下的修改：

【正】

1. I got up and washed my face. Then I ate my breakfast and went to the classroom.

2. She did some online shopping, and then she read a few pages of the book and fed her cat, then she made a phone call to her friend.

3. The dog barked. She began to run, but she fell over a stone and broke her head, so she cried.

具体的句子根据上下文的需要进行修改。

【误】The wind intensified it turned toward land.

本句的修改方案有如下几种。

添加逗号，后跟连词and：

【正】The wind intensified, and it turned toward land.

用句号隔开：

【正】The wind intensified. It turned toward land.

用分号隔开：

【正】The wind intensified; it turned toward land.

全句改写为：

【正】The wind that intensified turned toward land.

需要指出的是，有些学者把无标点句（fused sentence）和万能逗号句（comma splice）统称为粘连句（run-on sentence）。run-on这个词通常指两个相对独立的句子之间没有标点符号隔开，它与无标点句是一个概念，似乎与comma splice（指滥用逗号）没什么关系，极易造成误解，所以国内学界要慎用run-on sentence这个概念。

无标点句专项训练：

下列句子均没有标点符号或连接词，请按照本节学习的方法将之修改为正确的句子。

1. Trees lay on the side of the road they looked as if they had been pulled out of the ground by huge machines.

2. Every wall was smashed to rubble the only thing left of those houses was the land and the rocks from the rubble.

3. The town looked deserted the streets were so dark and empty that the only thing we could hear was the wind blowing.

4. We worked from dusk to dawn never had so many contracts been written in such a short time.

5. Money continued to flow in we started to live the life of the rich on weekends we ate at expensive restaurants.

6. The river extended beyond the mountains we saw the clouds merge with the water in the horizon.

7. Caffeine supplies the principal stimulant it increases the capacity for muscular and mental work without harmful reaction.

8. Like all good things in life, the drinking of coffee may be abused. Those having an idiosyncratic susceptibility to alkaloids should be temperate in the use of tea, coffee, or cocoa.

9. Some people cannot eat strawberries that would not be a valid reason for a general condemnation of strawberries.

第二节　万能逗号

逗号使用错误是英语写作中出现频率最高的错误之一。由于写作基础知识的缺失，我国学生在写作中最频繁使用的就是逗号与句号。其中任何地方的停顿、断句除了句号外，全部都使用逗号，产生"万能逗号（comma splice）"现象。

所谓"万能逗号"现象，指的是两个独立的句子之间本应该使用句号的，却使用了一个逗号。在万能逗号句中，虽然有一个逗号分隔两个独立的句子，但是在逗号的后面没有一个恰当的连接词连接，两个句子在句意上在逻辑上仍然是互为独立的。例如：

【误】

1. Kate stood up from the chair, went out of the door.

2. The man made an inspiring speech at the lecture hall, the audience was silent.

3. He threw a stone into the pond, a splash was heard, the ripples spread in all directions.

出现万能逗号错误的句子，可以按以下规则进行修改：

（1）使用句号断句。

（2）使用分号断句。

（3）使用逗号断句，逗号后的句子用连词and, or, nor, but, for, so, and yet等引导。

（4）将两个句子其一变成主句，另一个改成从句，用after, although, because, before, if, since, though, unless, until, when, where, and while连接。

（5）将其中一个句子变成一个状语性质的短语。

根据上面的修改原则，可以对上面的句子作如下修改。

【正】

1. Kate stood up from the chair and went out of the door.

2. The man made an inspiring speech at the lecture hall and the audience was silent.

3. He threw a stone into the pond. A splash was heard and the ripples spread in all directions.

根据全文的需要，在遵循语法规则与语言习惯、不改变原句中的逻辑关系的前提下，逗号误用的句子经过修改都可以通顺、完整、贴切地表达意义。例如：

【误】The boy got up late, he missed the classes.

本句的错误可通过如下几种方式进行修改。

添加连词：

【正】The boy got up late, and he missed the classes.

用句号断句：

【正】The boy got up late. He missed the classes.

用分号断句：

【正】The boy got up late; he missed the classes.

变成主从句：

【正】Because the boy got up late, so he missed the classes.

万能逗号句专项训练

一、下列句子都存在语病，判断其为无标点句还是万能逗号句。

1. Julie is a real hypochondriac when her stomach hurts, she is certain that she has a bleeding ulcer, and if she has a backache, she believes that she has cancer of the spine.

A. comma splice   B. fused sentence

2. My cat Buster loves to nap on warm appliances when he sleeps on top of the television, his tail swipes the screen like a windshield wiper.

A. comma splice   B. fused sentence

3. During English class, Anthony kept flirting with RaShaunda because his behavior was keeping Shenicka from understanding the lecture, Shenicka whacked him over the head with her heavy dictionary.

A. comma splice　　　　B. fused sentence

4. In preparation for the quiz, La'Mia studied comma splices and fused sentences until she thought her brain would burst, finally, she put away her notes, convinced that she would remember the rules even on her death bed.

A. comma splice　　　　B. fused sentence

5. At the back of the classroom, Nina sat with her arms crossed, glaring at her teacher, Mr. Beane, her body language indicated that English was her least favorite subject.

A. comma splice　　　　B. fused sentence

6. When Matt shaved his head, his mother worried that he had joined a cult the real reason for the bald head, however, was that Matt could get more attention and sympathy from girls who thought he was sick with a dread disease.

A. comma splice　　　　B. fused sentence

7. Mike loves to play computer games, especially Tomb Raider, he imagines that all of the villains are his problems, and he gets great satisfaction blasting them to bits.

A. comma splice　　　　B. fused sentence

8. Cindy's mumbling often gets her in trouble just the other day, in fact, her stylist misunderstood Cindy's instructions and dyed her hair blue after Cindy asked him to trim the ends.

A. comma splice　　　　B. fused sentence

9. Clyde knew that he should be saving money for next semester's tuition he spent every paycheck, however, on gold jewelry and expensive dinners for his greedy girlfriend Gloria.

A. comma splice　　　　B. fused sentence

10. At the campus coffee cart, Gini makes the best drinks her sweet cream latte, a blend of vanilla ice cream and espresso, will put on the pounds, but its

cool, smooth taste is worth a trip to the gym.

    A. comma splice   B. fused sentence

11. Josie, Don's Cairn terrier, will bark at anything that moves, squirrels, wind blown leaves, passing cars, and her own shadow will start her yapping.

    A. comma splice   B. fused sentence

12. Because his glasses were so thick, Quincy refused to get contacts, he worried that equally thick contact lenses would make him look like a bug-eyed space alien.

    A. comma splice   B. fused sentence

13. Madison believed that the best job in the universe would be to work as a crew member on the star ship Enterprise since this job existed only on television, Madison settled for clerking at a neighborhood comic book store that sold Star Trek memorabilia.

    A. comma splice   B. fused sentence

14. Michelle is terrified of spiders, so when she found one in the bathroom, she panicked, refusing to shower for three days to use the restroom, she drove to her neighborhood gas station.

    A. comma splice   B. fused sentence

15. When Jim threw his back out while helping his wife Nancy move the sofa, he feared the treatment the doctor would recommend, a week's worth of bed rest during the nicest week in April would certainly wreck Jim's golf plans.

    A. comma splice   B. fused sentence

16. Sima was so sleepy after her marathon studying session for calculus that she ordered a triple espresso before going to class once the caffeine kicked in, Sima knew that she wouldn't doze off on Dr. Ribley.

    A. comma splice   B. fused sentence

17. Rachel painstakingly ironed her linen shirt all the while, she was thinking how pointless this chore was since linen begins to wrinkle the moment after the last button is fastened.

    A. comma splice   B. fused sentence

18. Jeremiah likes to put peanut butter on his pancakes instead of syrup, the smell is appealing, but I wouldn't want to eat anything so sticky that early in the morning.

　　A. comma splice　　　　　B. fused sentence

19. Clarence couldn't believe that the hardware store was selling garden rakes for only $1.99 each when he brought home twenty of them, his wife Marie just shook her head and squeezed them into a garage stuffed full of her husband's other "good buys".

　　A. comma splice　　　　　B. fused sentence

20. Orange juice, toast, and cereal might be a healthy breakfast, but Ricardo always hits the snooze button on his alarm too many times all he can grab is a stale pastry and soda.

　　A. comma splice　　　　　B. fused sentence

二、判断下列句子的标点正误。

（　　）1. The roots of alienation go deep into the fabric of American social history, television's presence in the home encourages their unchecked growth.

（　　）2. AIDS tortures not only the body, it also damages the ego, the psyche, and the lifestyle of those it afflicts.

（　　）3. The lens focuses the light on the retina, this is the thin membrane covering the posterior surface of the eyeball.

（　　）4. Violence, of course, is rampant in the media yet it is usually set in some kind of moral context.

（　　）5. Solar energy could be harnessed to become the chief energy source on earth, and dangerous forms of energy could be eliminated.

三、给下列句子添加恰当的标点符号或改正已有的标点符号。

1. Most tarantulas live in the tropics but several species occur in the temperate zone and a few are common in the southern United States.

2. Typically, shopping centers are designed with one or more large department stores as magnets, these are located among the smaller stores to encourage impulse buying.

3. Both divorced mothers and divorced fathers have legitimate concerns but their

radically different viewpoints create poor communication between angry spouses.

4. All societies—whether primitive, agricultural, or industrial—use energy, they make things, they distribute things.

5. Congress passed the bill after long hours of debate there were strong convictions on both sides.

6. The railroads, highways, and cities that will spring up may divert attention, however, they cannot cover up society's decay.

7. I looked across the fire lane at a section that had been burned three weeks before and the ground was already covered with light green.

8. Homelessness itself is often the precipitating factor, for example, many pregnant women without homes are denied care because they constantly travel from one shelter to another.

第三节　垂悬及错位修饰

垂悬修饰指句子中一个分词短语作状语时，其逻辑主语与主句的主语不一致或指代不清，形成一仆二主，甚至一仆多主现象。含有垂悬修饰语的句子形成垂悬结构，类似于中文垂悬不定之意。垂悬修饰语也可以指修饰词（即定语）的错位导致其可以修饰多个目标词，造成理解上的歧义。错位修饰通常指副词（短语）、介词（短语）或形容词位置的错误，从而造成在结构上修饰错误的对象。

【例句】

1. Cooking in the kitchen, the delivery man arrived.

2. Sleeping in my orchard, a serpent stung me. (Hamlet, Act I, sc 5)

上面的两个例子中，第一句中谁在做饭，快递员还是本句未曾出现的主语？第二句中，是谁睡在桃园中，是"I"还是"the serpent"？由于修饰目标不明确，所以形成了垂悬修饰的情况。

垂悬修饰语通常有垂悬分词短语、垂悬动名词短语、垂悬不定式短语及垂悬副词（短语）；有时分词短语的逻辑主语与后面的句子主语不一致，导致状语垂悬。垂悬修饰语的修改原则是任何形式的修饰语的被修饰词应该具有唯一性。

现在分词垂悬：

【误】Having finished work, the door was lay open.

【正】Having finished work, he lay the door open and went out.

【误】Hoping to pass the exam, a lot of books were bought.

【正】Hoping to pass the exam, he bought a lot of books.

【误】Arriving at the top of the mountain, a pavilion was there.

【正】Arriving at the top of the mountain, they found a pavilion there.

【误】Cutting open the apple, a worm was inside.

【正】Cutting open the apple, he saw a worm inside.

【误】Climbing half way up the tree, some squirrels were nibbling the nuts.

【正】Climbing half way up the tree, he saw some squirrels were nibbling the nuts.

【误】Reading the regulations, the dog was not let in.

【正】Reading the regulations, he didn't let in his dog.

【误】Working harder than ever, this job still proved to be too much for him to handle.

【正】Working harder than ever, he still found this job too much for him to handle.

【正】Although he worked harder than ever, this job still proved to be too much for him to handle.

动名词垂悬：

【误】After finishing his homework, the teacher let the boy go.

【正】The teacher let the boy go after he finished his homework.

【误】By having a look at the girl, she attracted his attention.

【正】By having a look at the girl, he was attracted by her.

【误】After being scolded, the mother let the boy do his homework by himself.

【正】After being scolded, the boy was made to do his homework by himself.

不定式结构垂悬：

【误】To become a good teacher, hard work and patience is needed.

【正】To become a good teacher, you need to work hard and be patient.

Hard work and patience is needed if you want to become a good teacher.

【误】To start the program, funding is needed.

【正】To start the program, you need to apply for funding.

Funding is needed if you want to start the program.

错位修饰语：

修饰语的错位现象通常指副词（短语）、介词（短语）或形容词位置的错误，从而造成在结构上可以修饰一个或多个成分；其修改方法是尽量将修饰语放在被修饰成分的接近的地方。如果以上句子里被修饰的词根本不存在，则修饰成分悬空成为垂悬修饰语。请看下列例句：

I ran after the thief in slippers.（谁穿拖鞋，我还是小偷？）

The tiger looked at the wolf in the cage.（谁在笼子里，老虎还是狼？）

【误】Students who study rarely get bad grades.（谁没有考好，是不学习的同学还是认真学习的同学？）

【正】Students who rarely study get bad grades.

Students who study get bad grades rarely .

这类句子的修改原则是修饰哪个词就紧挨着哪个词，否则就会造成歧义，带来理解上的困难，同时还要确保那个被修饰的词在句子里是存在的。

垂悬结构专项训练

一、下列每组句子中有一句包含垂悬结构，找出正确的那句并解释理由。

（　　）1. A. Having misunderstood the assignment, I received a low grade on my paper.

B. Having misunderstood the assignment, my paper got a low grade.

（　　）2. A. Returning after a year out of the country, my cat did not even know me.

B. When I returned after a year out of the country, my cat did not even know me.

(　　) 3. A. Having been marinated overnight, you may now cook the meat.

B. Having been marinated overnight, the meat is now ready to be cooked.

(　　) 4. A. As the squirrel steadfastly replaced the lost acorns, I marveled at its determination and hard work.

B. Steadfastly replacing the lost acorns, I marveled at the squirrel's determination and hard work.

(　　) 5. A. When I was in high school, English was my favorite subject.

B. When in high school, English was my favorite subject.

(　　) 6. A. Because the spelunkers were covered with the mud from the cave, my mother would not let them come into the house.

B. Covered with the mud from the cave, my mother would not let the spelunkers come into the house.

(　　) 7. A. To avoid having your cake fall, you need to adjust the baking temperature for altitude.

B. To avoid having your cake fall, the baking temperature should be adjusted for altitude.

(　　) 8. A. Meeting my husband in California, I suggested I drive home with him.

B. Meeting my husband in California, he suggested I drive home with him.

(　　) 9. A. To be sure we get the seats we want, we purchase our tickets a year in advance.

B. To be sure we get the seats we want, our tickets are purchased a year in advance.

(　　) 10. A. Seen from miles away, Mount Timpanogos looks impressive.

B. Seen from miles away, we are impressed with Mount Timpanogos.

二、下面的句子中都有一个垂悬或错位修饰错误，请将它们找出来并改正错误。

1. Looking up to the sky, some clouds were floating up above their heads.

2. After cleaning the room, my dog wanted to take a walk.

3. Flying in the sky, I shot the bird.

4. At the age of seven, my mother gave birth to my brother.

5. While having an English class, Jim phoned me.

6. While driving, my tire went flat.

7. Swimming in the river, the boat floats away.

8. While sleeping, the pet dog ran loose and never came back.

第四节　句子成分残缺

残缺句指的是没有主语或没有谓语的句子，也可以用来指意义不完整或其他成分缺失的句子。请看下列句子：

He rose from the chair. And went away.（缺少主语）

You must study harder. Or you won't pass the final exam.（意义不完整）

A plane in the sky.（缺少谓语）

Two wolves after the butcher for a long time.（缺少谓语）

缺少主语：

【误】How to make a kite?

How to say that in English?

I am an out-going guy. Like to listen to the music and like to play the basketball.

They got up early. And started for the park.

【正】How can I make a kite?

Do you know how to say that in English?

I am an out-going guy. I like to listen to the music and to play the basketball.

They got up early and started for the park.

缺少谓语：

【误】The audience in the auditorium.

The dog across the lawn.

How many people in the room?

A lot of noises in the next room.

【正】The audience were in the auditorium.

The dog ran across the lawn.

How many people are there in the room?

A lot of noises can be heard in the next room.

意义不完整：

【误】We have to study further. For we must follow the most recent development of the subject that we focus on.

【正】We have to study further, for we must follow the most recent development of the subject that we focus on.

【误】Those people who are opposed to the above-mentioned opinion. They think that this method will lead to nowhere.

【正】Those people who are opposed to the above-mentioned opinion think that this medod will lead to nowhere.

误用引导词：

【误】We went to the park. Where we took a walk.

【正】We went to the park where we took a walk.

第五节　平行结构

英语中的平行结构与中文中的排比句有些相似之处但又不完全相同。英语中的平行结构可以是互相独立的句子，也可以是句子内部几个具有同等地位、结构相同的短语，有时还可以是几个并列的词语。平行结构必须遵循平行、对等和一致原则，即：

（1）功能上具有同等地位，即平行。

（2）结构上相同或相似，即结构要对等。

（3）描述对象相同，即描述主体必须一致。

平行结构的特点是气势磅礴、韵律相似、节奏感强、短小精悍，多维度描写目标词。使用平行结构可以用来加强语句的气势、渲染氛围，同时由于具有相似的音韵节奏，赏心悦目，朗朗上口，语句显得优美，容易被读者接受。再次，并列的结构可以用很短的几个字词句，把事物的各个侧面描述出来，读者在极短的时间内，用欣赏的心态，就能比较全面地了解事物。平行结构与并列句的区别在于，并列句通常是不需要结构相似的句子而且还必须用连接词and, or, but等连接起来；平行结构不一定是若干句子，通常不需要连接词，作为独立结构存在，用以说明主题的某一个方面，可以用逗号，分号甚至句号隔开。

不平行的结构本质上就是并列句，它也许没有语法错误，但没有平行结构的艺术效果。要想达到排山倒海一样的气势、诗歌一样的韵律，就得使用平等结构。请看下列句子：

【不平行】Being a teacher, you must make clear what to teach, how you will teach it and how your students are going to learn it.

上句是通顺的，意思表达也是完整无误的；但它不是平行句，因为what to teach是动词不定式短语，how you will teach it and how your students are going to learn it则是宾语从句，三者结构不是一样的。如果想使用平行结构，可以考虑改为：

【平行】

1. Being a teacher, you must make clear what you will teach, how you will teach it and how your students will to learn it.

2. Being a teacher, you must make clear what to teach, how to teach it and how to learn it on the part of your students.

【不平行】We should be clear what we will do, how to do it, and how we can gain the expected result.

【平行】We should be clear what we will do, how we will do it, and how we can gain theexpected result.

【平行】We should be clear what to do, how to do it, and how to gain the expected result.

【不平行】Teachers in a research institute have fewer students than in a university.

【平行】Teachers in a research institute have fewer students than those in a university.

从上面的例子中不难看出，平行结构的核心要素，是结构上的相同，结构上不相同的句子一般都被认为是并列句。如果不追求强烈的语气，并列句也能把事物说清楚、说完整。但是如果想写平行结构，一定做到"平行、对等、一致"。

平行结构通常有句式平行和内部成分平行两种情况。

句式平行：

（1）I came, I saw, I conquered.

（2）Ask not what your country can do for you; ask what you can do for your country.

（3）He lived for the people; he died for the people.

成分平行：

句子、短语、单词都可以构成平行结构。

（1）Confucious was a great educator, a great thinker, a great philosopher and a great statesman in Chinese history.

（2）She is a white, rich and pretty girl.

（3）Belle was a timid, talented, and creative person.

（4）The boy is silent, hard-working and helpful.

介词、冠词短语构成平行：

（1）The ambassador used to work in Germany, in France and in Britain.

（2）The people came from the east, from the west, from the north and from the south.

（3）All the Chinese people are celebrating the same event, in Beijing, in Xinjiang, in Hainan and in Shanghai.

（4）When we practice our sun salutations in Los Angeles, we welcome the same sun that is greeted and admired in Shanghai, in Sydney, in London, in Calcutta, in Osaka and in Buenos Aires.

试析下列结构。

【不平行】At Wal-Mart on Saturday, I bought Q-Tips, apples, spinach, and got a roasted chicken for lunch.

解析："got a roasted chicken for lunch."与清单中其他成分不对等，可以改为：

【平行】At Wal-Mart on Saturday, I bought Q-Tips, apples, spinach, and roasted chicken.

【不平行】To forget the past means turning traitor.

解析：主语中的动词不定式与表语中的动名词短语不对等，不能构成平行。

【平行】To forget the past means to turn traitor.

Forgetting the past means turning traitor.

【不平行】The HR director took responsibility for hiring, firing, and recruits.

解析：recruits与前面的hiring, firing 形式上不对等、不平行。

【平行】The HR director took responsibility for hiring, firing, and recruiting.

【不平行】The poverty-relieving program in the area raised money to pay for training courses in farming, livestock raising and company employees.

解析：句末company employees 与前面的farming, livestock raising不对等、不平行。

【平行】The poverty-relieving program in the area raised money to pay for training courses in farming, livestock raising and other work skills.

【不平行】At school, she learned to speak English and writing good essays.

解析：writing good essays 与to speak English 形式上不对等，应改为to write good essays.

【平行】At school, she learned to speak English and to write good essays.

同一个句子中有几个并列的动词不定式作宾语，有些人习惯所有的动词不定式共用第一个to。例如：

At school, she learned to listen, speak, read and write.

从语法结构上看，这种并列句是完全正确的，符合简洁的原则，但它们不是平行结构。但是有些时候为了强调是必须使用平行结构的。例如：

（1）Some principles are applied in the fighting of the virus: early detection, early diagnosis, early isolation and early treatment.

（2）We work hard to find a good job, to make more money, to make our families happier and to be in better service of our country.

平行结构专项训练

一、下列句子中存在不平行错误，找到它们并改正。

1. My uncle Julius likes bagels, lox, and eating chicken salad.

2. Bill not only runs five miles every day, he consumes eight thousand calories.

3. Jose's daughter will either attend Harvard, or she plans to go to the Standford.

4. Fatima's knowledge of accounting is greater than Farah.

5. Stephen King's book reviews were as positive as Asimov.

6. The house sitter lost the keys, neglected the dogs, and she also trashed the kitchen.

7. Andrew was both an industrious student, and he was also an excellent athlete.

8. She was not only beautiful but also a spoiled child.

9. A math book with practice problems and having a good index is useful.

10. Customers may climb the stairs, ride the escalator, or taking the elevator.

11. Jake knew he had to run or stayed to face the consequences.

12. To sleep and eating were his main occupations.

13. Either he should do it or let me do it.

14. Her ambition was both to act in movies and writing a book about her experiences.

15. Mary likes to paint, sew, and playing the piano is another hobby.

16. That mask will not only scare Billy but also the cat.

二、判断下列各组句子是否平行，在平行的句子前打T，在不平行的句子前打F。

(　) 1a. The employee was conscientious, devoted, and he worked hard.

(　) 1b. The employee was conscientious, devoted, and hard-working.

(　) 2a. The camp has several fields for games and swimming in the lake.

(　) 2b. The camp has several fields for games and a swimming area in the lake.

(　) 3a. Andy wanted neither the assignment at Columbus nor the job at Toledo.

(　) 3b. Andy wanted neither the assignment at Columbus nor to be sent to

Toledo.

( ) 4a. Eve is an excellent tennis player, serving fast and being good at volleying.

( ) 4b. Eve is an excellent tennis player, having a fast serve and a good volley.

( ) 5a. She was both a good skier and liked to play basketball.

( ) 5b. She was both a good skier and a fine basketball player.

( ) 6a. He told me to shut up, mind my own business, and leave him alone.

( ) 6b. He told me to shut up, mind my own business, and to leave him alone.

第六节 语言不简练

英语中wordiness就是指句子写得很啰唆，redundancy本意是多余、冗余。在写作理论实践中两个概念可以互换，不提倡加以区分。不难看出，和中文里一样，英语句子讲究简洁、精练。语句不精练，英语写作实践中称为redundancy，即不必要的重复（unnecessary repetition）。还有一种情况是句子太啰唆，明明话说完了，还写一大堆话，英语对应的词是wordy。这两种情况在写作实践中为同一概念，统称为语句不简练。

中外文学名家的作品，文字洗练，每个句子都经过千锤百炼，经得住推敲，以致成为经典。对初学者来说，出现语句不精练，主要还是对单词的内涵和外延没有完全了解，没有经过仔细琢磨与推敲，拿来即用，盲目堆砌。随着词汇量的增长、阅读量的加大、写作风格的成熟、思维逻辑能力的提升，这些问题将逐步得到改善。

使用重复的、多余的词汇，不但对增加文章的文采没有帮助，反而会降低文章的可读性。英语写作实践中，慎用冷字偏字，切忌使用自己没有把握的字、词、句。

那么如何才能避免不必要的重复和空洞堆砌呢？有一条原则是任何时候都应该遵守的，即尽量使用常见的、简短的词，尽量使用简单的句子、短句子，能不用修饰性的从句就不要用从句。语句累赘冗长，必然影响意思的表达，增加读者理解的难度。我们在学习写作时以下几点需要注意。

（1）能用一个词的时候不用两个词。

（2）能用简短的单词就不用太长的单词。

（3）能用一个单词表达的意思不用从句表达。

（4）同样的概念不表达两次。

（5）能用主动语态时尽量不用被动语态。

句子不简练通常包括名词前的定语重复、副词或形容词对所修饰动词本身意思的重复、修饰性从句的重复、堆砌。过度堆砌造成概念重叠、逻辑混乱，降低了文章的可读性。

句子不简练，可以表现为以下几种形式。

其一，不必要的重复。

A. 意思重复

free gift（礼物有收费的吗？）

foreign imports（外国来的不都是进口的吗？）

clearly obvious（意思重复）

true fact（事实都是真实的）

brief summary（summary都是简要的综述）

basic fundamentals（基本原则还不基本吗？）

end result（result是最终结果了，还加end干什么？）

sudden crisis（难道危机到来自己还会提前通知？）

close proximity（proximity本身就是近似、大约的意思，加close多余）

【Redundancy】Justin is a friendly and amicable guy.

amicable 就是friendly的意思，应该删除。

【Brevity】Justin is a friendly guy.

【Redundancy】It was a fine sunny day.

fine与sunny说的是同一种天气。

【Brevity】It was a fine day.

【Redundancy】The work she did was tiring exhausting work.

tiring与exhausting意思是重复的，需要重新组织语言，使意思表达得更清晰。

【Brevity】She was tired with her work.

B. 修饰语的重复

【Redundancy】She worked for thirty years as a teacher and librarian in the field of education in some public schools.

in some public schools本身就是干教育，何须再说一句文绉绉的in the field of education?

【Brevity】She worked for thirty years as a teacher and librarian in some public schools.

【Reduncancy】Despite the fact that she was feeling ill, she came to the conclusion that she would go to class.

本句中，生病与得出结论因果关系不强，是多余的话。

【Brevity】Despite feeling ill, she decided to go to work.

【Redundancy】The reason why he came to Douglas College was because it was inexpensive in price.

本句中，reason, why, because意义重叠，inexpensive本身表达的就是in price。

【Brevity】He came to Douglas College because it was inexpensive.

【Redundancy】I think maybe I might possibly have met them all.

本句中，I think, maybe, might possibly 意义重叠。

【Brevity】I possibly have met them all.

【Redundancy】In my opinion, I think the study of sociology is very fascinating.

本句中，in my opinion和 I think意思是相同的；the study of sociology不妥。sociology 是一门学科名称，本身就需要学习的；fascinating 的意思是very interesting, 可不加very。

【Brevity】Sociology is fascinating.

其二，语言啰唆、累赘

请看如下几例：

small in size

few in number

red in color

tall in height

【Wordiness】We had a stay in the city during the outbreak of the virus that was a nightmare.

【Brevity】We had a nightmarish stay in the city during the virus outbreak.

【Wordiness】I enjoy getting my nourishment by way of fried foods.

【Brevity】I enjoy eating fried foods.

【Wordiness】Being troubled by long-time stress, he set about on a plan which resulted in the fact that he went to the beach.

【Brevity】He went to the beach in order to shuffle off the stress.

【Wordiness】It seemed that he was always occupied by his work, hence consequently no time was spent with his family to be in their company.

【Brevity】He was too busy with his work and had no time with his family.

【Wordiness】On the date of August 28th 1963, Dr. Martin Luther King, Jr. delivered a speech that brought different nationalities together in the hope to stop discrimination and live equally in peace no matter what color you were.

【Brevity】On August 28th 1963, Dr. Martin Luther King, Jr. delivered a speech that brought different nationalities together in the hope to stop discrimination.

【Wordiness】The teacher became increasingly frustrated with the naughty student who acted in a wild, disorderly manner.

【Brevity】The teacher became increasingly frustrated with the naughty student.

【Wordiness】George, after thirty years of work in the factory, was very glad to retire and no longer go to his job.

【Brevity】George, after thirty years of work in the factory, was very glad to retire.

其三，在一些固定句型中，语句不精练的情况频发。如there is/are结构、it is...结构中。如果结构不能十分贴切地表达句意，还是直接使用主谓结构更好。

【Redundancy】There is a famous author who lives in our neighbourhood.

【Brevity】A famous author lives in our neighbourhood.

【Redundancy】There are many people who play computer games online.

【Brevity】Many people play computer games online.

【Redundancy】There are some animals that thrive in arctic temperatures.

【Brevity】Some animals thrive in arctic temperatures.

【Redundancy】It is rarely the case that people refuse to help.

【Brevity】People rarely refuse to help.

【Redundancy】It is a fact that most of us like to be praised.

【Brevity】Most of us like to be praised.

试析下列句子。

【Redundancy】After the conclusion of the concert we left.

after本身就表示结束，conclusion意思重叠。

【Brevity】We left after the concert.

【Redundancy】We appreciate any and all suggestions.

本句中，any或者all都是排他的，都能表示全体，只能选择其一。

【Brevity】We appreciate any suggestions.

【Redundancy】We are looking for a solution at the present moment.

没有at the present moment这种说法，不如老老实实地直接说now。

【Brevity】We are looking for a solution now.

【Redundancy】He came by means of a car.

英语中by car已经为大众所普遍接受，不存在by means of a car这个说法，虽然它是符合语法规则的。

【Brevity】He came by car.

【Redundancy】Due to the fact that he called, we waited.

Because比due to the fact that...更简洁。

【Brevity】Because he called, we waited.

【Redundancy】The meeting is for the purpose of discussing plans.

简单的话要简单地说，for the purpose of+动名词，不如直接用动词不定式。

【Brevity】The meeting is to discuss plans.

【Redundancy】He is a man who is admired.

如此简单的句子不需要用定语从句，不能把简单的问题复杂化。

【Brevity】He is admird.

【Redundancy】They lived in a place where no trees grew.

删除in a place后更像一个正常句子。

【Brevity】They lived where no trees grew.

【Redundancy】He said this in order to help you.

这句话不是书面语，不需要这么说，还是简洁点好。

【Brevity】He said this to help you.

【Redundancy】In spite of the fact that she agreed, she was sad.

简简单单一句话不需要说得这么费劲，应该直接用although/though。

【Brevity】Although she agreed, she was sad.

【Redundancy】She rarely ever speaks to a large group.

rarely ever就是rarely，除非需要特别强调，否则一般不这么用。

【Brevity】She rarely speaks to a large group.

【Redundancy】The fact is that you are the right candidate.

过于复杂，不需使用the fact is that。

【Brevity】You are the right candidate.

【Redundancy】I spoke with him yesterday, which was when he called.

说得很累，听起来很费劲，简单点说话者听话者都轻松了。

【Brevity】I spoke with him yesterday when he called.

【Redundancy】I like all sports with the exception of boxing.

with the exception of是书面语，其意思本身就是except。如果不是正式书面语的文章还是简单点好。

【Brevity】I like all sports except boxing.

语句不简练专项训练

一、下列短语中包含有多余的形容词、副词或名词，找到它们并改正。

free gift, sad lament, brief summary, fundamental basis, safe haven, close intimates, close scrutiny, human artifact, sudden impulse, Jewish rabbi, true fact, consensus of opinion, two opposites, new innovation, unexpected surprise, empty void, unimportant triviality, end result, past history,wealthy millionaire, famous celebrity, rejected outcast, vast majority, futrue ahead, completey unanimous, more better, currently at this time, now pending, present incumbent

二、下列动词短语中包含有多余的修饰词，找到它们并改正。

advance forward, continue on, cooperate together, enter into, join together, leave from, lower down, proceed forward, raise up, retreat back, return back, revert back, share in common, share together.

三、下列各句不够精练，请找出不恰当的部分并予以删除。

1. The famous NBA player is high in height.

2. We were tired and exhausted after the long climb to the high top of the mountain.

3. He was happy and joyful about the great free gift.

4. Due to the fact that the epidemic swept across the country, many communities and airports were locked down.

5. In the summer season, many locals like to picnic in the People's Park.

6. On January 14, in the middle of the winter, the weather was freezing cold.

7. In order to get the true facts of the case, the lawyer interviewed 4 witnesses.

8. Furthermore, he also finished reading over 100 books that are related to the topic.

9. The computer is sitting on top of the table.

10. The army advanced forward.

四、下列句子有不精练的地方，找出来并改正。

1. I returned back to my room after the meeting was over.

_____

_____

2. Please repeat again what you said.

_____

_____

3. The situation is very serious in nature.

_____

_____

4. It was a story that was difficult to tell.

_____

_____

5. The roof of the house is red in color.

_____

_____

6. Here is a brief summary of the hour's story.

_____

_____

7. Our neighbor who lives in the house next door has been the recipient of an invitation to the governor's ball.

_____

_____

8. Aluminium is a metal that is very light in weight.

_____

_____

第二编
英语文体写作

第一章　英语的文体与写作

第一节　英语的文体

英语中主要有记叙文（narrative）、描写文（descriptive）、议论文（persuasive/argumentative）和说明文（expository）四种写作文体。国外少数学者主张将英语文体划分为十几种，并在四大文体之外提出了对比—对照文体（comparison-contrast）、原因—结果文体（cause-effect）等文体；但这些所谓的文体明显是四大文体中常用的写作手法（writing devices），其划分缺乏理论依据，没有得到学界主流观点的认可，我国学界不予采纳。

作者通常根据自己的写作意图、写作内容来决定采用什么文体。写作的过程就是利用自己掌握的材料，从主题的不同侧面将它们组织成相应的段落，分层次、分步骤进行创作。每一个段落，即主题的某一个侧面需要有一个主题句；每个段落支撑句的功能就是论证、说明、解释本段落主题句。正文部分中所有的段落都是中心思想的支撑段。

英语写作中，文章的第一段（引言段）第一句通常应该能够引起读者的阅读兴趣，这句话在英语里叫hook或者interest getter，相当于中文里说的悬念。开篇第一句设置一个悬念是写作中常见的手法。全文的中心思想句（thesis statement）应该在引言段中表述出来，通常出现在引言段的最后一句。中心思想句的作用是总领全文，后面的每个段落都要为这个中心思想服务，围绕着主题思想来写。最后一段叫结尾段，结尾段的作用是总结并结束全文。通常情况下结尾段应该总结前文并呼应引言段的中心思想，英语中叫restatement，即重申主题。重申主题时不是把中心思想句照抄一遍，而是根据正文中的内容对主题进行升华。议论文中的重申主题句后面还应该有一句

call to action（行动倡议）。

通常情况下，"五段式"是英语写作中最流行、采用范围最广的写作模式，是我们学习写作时最应该掌握的目标。同时，还存在一个简化的写作格式，即"三段式"。它主要是为初学者设计的一种简易版的写作模式，以英语为母语的国家有时也采用这种写作模式对中低年级学生进行写作启蒙教学。从"三段式"的形式上不难看出，它是幼稚的、不成熟的；这样的写作在形式上是不丰满的、内容上是不深入完整的，势必导致叙事不彻底、不全面、不深入，让读者感到说服力不强、过于笼统、描写不细腻生动、对论点的支撑也不十分到位。尽管有这些不足，但"三段式"仍然不失为一个不错的过渡性写作模式。在我国的英语写作中"三段式"十分流行。我国中小学的英语书面表达、大学低年级的写作习作普遍使用"三段式"模式。

第二节　文体写作

英语写作分为自选题写作和命题写作。

在自选题写作中，首先要做的是要明确写作目的。写什么样的文章就应当选择对应的文体。譬如，写一段自己的经历就应当选择记叙文，论述一个话题就应该选择议论文，一篇游记最好采用描写文，一篇介绍性的文字则使用说明文。

命题写作中，如果题目已经给出则可以直接构思文章。但是，在大学阶段的写作实践中出题者通常是只给出一个写作提示或写作范围，而不是直接布置题目。这种提示或范围在英语写作学科中有一个专门的名称，叫prompt（提示）。这种作文通常需要作者根据提供的写作范围拟定一个题目（title）。题目应当针对具体事物、事件和论点，主题不可涉及太广，太宽泛了初学者一般很难驾驭。例如：

Prompt: You've been learning English for many years and still outside the door of the language and you feel frustrated at this. Please write an essay to analyze your problem and find a solution to it.

以上是一个写作范围，作者需要根据自己学习英语时遇到的痛点和难点自拟一个题目。

学习英语会有这样或那样的问题，发音、听力、语法、阅读、写作等方面会在不同阶段出现各种困难和问题。我们不可能也没必要写出学习上的所有问题，可以选择其中一个最关键的问题来写，如背单词的重要性。例如：

The Importance of Building a Large Vocabulary

Outline:

Ⅰ. Introduction	
A. Many problems may arise in the process of English learning.	Hook
B. In my opinion, to build a large vocabulary is of vital importance to learning English well.	Thesis statement
Ⅱ. Body Paragraph 1	
A. Short of words	Detail 1
B. Can't understand sentences when reading	Detail 2
C. Not able to write it	Detail 3
D. Can't make myself understood	Detail 4
E. Word choice mistakes	Detail 5
Ⅲ. Body Paragraph 2	
A. My teacher's advice	Detail 1
B. Borrowing books from the library	Detail 2
C. Making progress	Detail 3
Ⅳ. Conclusion	
A. A summary	Generalization
B. Now I know what I needed was to memorize more words by reading. And I made it.	Restatement of the thesis, but not the same sentence

首先是草创（draft/draught）阶段。根据以上提纲可以进行文章的创作：

Many problems may arise in the process of English learning. In my opinion, to build a large vocabulary is of vital importance to learning English well.

A year ago, whenever I tried to put pen to paper, I ran short of words to express myself. Every time I opened a book and set about the work of reading a page, I experienced a hard time making sense of the meaning of the sentences. When it comes to the question of writing essays, I couldn't write them even if I knew the pictures were right there in my mind. When I communicated with others in English, I found I could not make myself understood. When I handed in my papers to my teacher, he would find many mistakes concerning word choice, sentence patterns and errors of tense. I often wondered why this was so, what happened to my learning of English.

Later, my teacher advised me to read more. So I borrowed some English short stories from the school library. My English ability began to improve after I finished reading a few of them.

Now I feel at ease with reading and writing and can communicate with my foreign teachers quite well. I begin to know what I needed in the past was to memorize more words by reading. And I made it.

文章写出来之后还需要经过校对（proofreading）、修改（revise/rewriting）和编辑（editing）。这个过程包括对标题、正文字号、字体和行距等的编辑。同时，还包括纠正大小写、标点错误，以及检查段落的换行、单词的移行规则有没有错误。做完这一切就可以打印或者发布了。

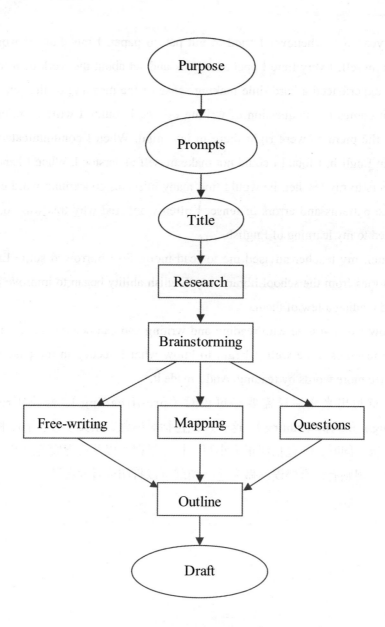

第二章　记叙文

第一节　什么是英语的记叙文

记叙文，顾名思义就是叙述一段个人的或他人的经历，即讲故事。记叙文通常是以第一人称叙述，有时也可以第三人称叙述。随着故事情节的发展，读者好似看到发生在身边的事情，犹如身临其境，尤其是使用第一人称叙述时可以让读者产生强烈共鸣，仿佛自己也是故事中的人物一样。

一个故事的讲述通常由故事背景、人物、事件、起因、过程和结果等要素构成，可以归纳为时间（when）、地点（where）、人物（who）、事件（what）、原因（why）和结果（how）。叙述通常以时间顺序（chronological order/time order）安排故事情节的发展。与我国语文课中的记叙文不同的是，英语中的记叙文以文中人物的对话（dialogue）为其显著特征。对话能反映出故事所处历史时代的特色、人物的身份地位、受教育程度等，人物的原话无论粗俗或高雅、激扬或低沉、阳光或消极，都能通过其语言鲜明、突出地表现人物性格，衬托故事情节的发展。对话以直接引语的形式出现在记叙文中。

所有的故事都是人与人之间或人与环境之间的互动。这种互动的关系可以是母慈子孝、父爱如山，也可以是两情相悦，但是真正感人至深的故事一般都是人与人之间的冲突或者人与社会环境、自然环境之间的冲突，进而演绎令人唏嘘的悲剧故事、惊天动地的爱情故事或者可歌可泣的英雄故事。在记叙文中，事件或人物的冲突（conflict）构成故事的高潮（climax）。与小说不同的是，记叙文的冲突需要在文中得到解决，读者在读完文章后好奇心理得到满足，悬念得到解决。有时作者在结尾段暗示一些寓意，揭示某些道理，与引言段中的主题思想相呼应，或者分析一下事件的成因、结果及影响。结尾段落的议论性语句不影响把全文定义为记叙文。

记叙文与小说最大的区别在于，小说不一定需要一个结局，可以给读者留下无限的想象空间，任由读者思绪展开、发展，可以有无数种假设与遐想。不同时代、不同的读者可能会对小说情节、人物做出不同的解读。小说不需要遵守任何格式，可以随着故事情节的发展而任由作者自由发挥。

广义上，我们常见的传记、轶事、报告文学、故事、小说、新闻报道等都属于记叙文的范畴。

第二节　记叙文的写作

记叙文通常采用"五段式"写作形式，初学写作可以使用"三段式"。

记叙文的正文部分通常有三个或三个以上的段落，每个段落都必须围绕文章的中心思想来写，涵盖时间（when）、地点（where）、人物（who）、事件（what）、原因（why）和结果（how）。正文部分叙述具体的事件及过程，描写应生动、具体，如人物要写是老人还是孩子，长什么样、穿什么衣服、什么表情、什么声音等；农作物要具体写是玉米、高粱、水稻还是小麦等；植物的描写要具体描绘其形态、叶子形状以及花的形状、颜色及味道；动物要具体到是狗、猫、老虎、狮子还是狼，要刻画它们的形态、眼光、动作以及叫声。总之，要详略得当，注重细节，服务情节，完整地讲一个故事。故事情节的叙述也要采用细腻的笔触，人物的一颦一笑，心理活动的每一个细节都要花笔墨进行描述，把画面呈现在读者眼前，像放电影一样让读者有身临其境的感觉。故事就是由一系列的情节构成的，情节是由画面呈现的，记叙文的写作中，情节的描述要有画面感。

记叙文的结尾段通常有一个经验总结，也可以提出本文有什么教育意义，英语中叫moral。

第三节 记叙文的写作格式

与任何文体一样，记叙文的写作也需要遵守一定的格式（format），即"五段式"和"三段式"。记叙文的创作需要先酝酿思路，撰写提纲。提纲对文章的写作能起到事半功倍的效果。固定的格式虽然对思路有一定的限制，但总体不影响写作中创新性的发挥，在一定的范围内仍可以挥洒自如，创作出不朽的作品。

一、"五段式"文章

英语中的写作基本上都遵守"五段式"的格式，它是主流的写作模式。记叙文通常有一个标题及三个部分，即引言、正文、结尾段，同时还必须有一个中心思想贯穿始终。所有的段落都必须为这个中心思想服务，围绕这个中心思想来发挥。正文部分的段落称为支撑段，每个支撑段都描写主题的某一个侧面。

"五段式"提纲：

Title		
Introductory Paragraph	Hook	
	Thesis statement	
Body Paragraph 1	Body Paragraph 2	Body Paragraph 3
Detail 1	Detail 1	Detail 1
Detail 2	Detail 2	Detail 2
Detail 3	Detail 3	Detail 3
Concluding Paragraph	Say your thesis differently	
	Lesson readers learn from the narrative	

二、"三段式"文章

所谓"三段式"结构文章，主要指针对传统的"五段论"结构文章的一种简化的结构，其目的就是解决非母语国家学生学习英语写作时遇到的困难。只含有三段的文章基本上满足了文章的最低要求，能包含文章的各种要素。

"三段式"的文体是各非英语国家在进行初级英语写作教学时普遍采用的写作格式。其中，引言段和结尾段有时候可以只有数句甚至一句，也能形成一段。正文部分也不再要求三段，而是一个大段。这样的写作模式结构简单，大大降低了写作难度，对于习惯于只写一大段的中学和大学低年级初学写作的同学来说起到了启蒙的作用，对essay（文章）有了初步的认识。

"三段式"文章是极简风格的文章。必须指出的是，"三段式"文章的风格是幼稚的和不成熟的，是不能满足复杂的叙事目的的，只能作为一个过渡性的写作训练，学习写作还是要以能够写出一篇成熟的文章为目标的。

目前，我国大中小学英语写作中的书面表达都属于"三段式"文体的写作。

"三段式"提纲：

Title	
I. Introductory paragraph	A. Background information
	B. Thesis statement
II. Body	A. Supporting detail
	B. Supporting detail
	C. Supporting detail
III. Concluding paragraph	A. Summary
	B. Restatement of the thesis

第四节 范文学习

【范文1】

Pleasure-seeking Trip to the Beach

（1）As the proverb says, "All work and no play make Jack a dull boy." People need a rest every now and then after long hours of work day after day. An escape from worldly matters for relaxation to relieve the stress is a good idea for your mental health and for better work as well. Driven by some kind of impulse of an escape from the endless lessons and homework, I decided to embark on a pleasure-seeking trip to the beach with a group of friends for a refresh last Sunday.

（2）On approaching the beach, we felt so relaxed and happy. The air was so fresh and the landscapes were beautiful. The vast sea extended into the blue of the sky at the horizontal line. We felt that we became part of the nature and forgot all worldly worries.

（3）There were crowds of tourists on the beach when we arrived; some of them were walking on the white sand or wading in the shallow sea water, others were taking photos. Laughters could be heard far and near.

（4）At one entrance, our attention was caught by a sign which read, "scuba-diving". I heard of stories about diving and saw many pictures of divers swimming like a fish among lovely sea creatures of all shapes and colors. We all agreed to have a try.

（5）We took a brief course in safety instruction and some training in diving skills. We learned how to wave signals to communicate with others in the water and how to use the equipments before we started out. The next minute we found ourselves on a steamboat into the ocean and somewhere at sea the boat stopped. I tried hard to discharge my uneasiness and moved to one side of the boat at the order of the instructor; air tank on back and mask and goggles on face, I plucked up my courage and thrust myself into the blue water at one jump. I was soon enjoying myself in a wonderful underwater world with different types of fish swimming in front of me as if I was invisible, some of which I had never seen before. It was great experience becoming one of them and part of the ocean. The sea definitely looked beautiful with its diverse marine life and the colorful coral reefs. It really amazed me to realize that there are thousands of creatures living peacefully under the sea.

（6）It was indeed so peaceful down there. Everything was so quiet. All I could hear was only my breath… breathing in，breathing out，while enjoying the mysterious underwater world and its inhabitants around me.

（7）Two weeks after my underwater exploration, we took final exams of the term, which turned out to be a great success. I got A's for all my courses. I enjoyed the visit to the beach and it helped a lot in my schoolwork.

【点评】

本文以时间为线索，步步展开，以生动的语言叙述了作者和朋友们一起去海边游玩的故事。第一自然段为引言段；自然段二、三、四、五、六为支撑段，为过程描写，是故事的主体部分，为中心思想提供支撑，丰富主题；第七自然段是结尾段。

Paragraph 1：

引言段以谚语开篇，第二句设置悬念"日复一日的工作需要时常放松一下"（People need a rest every now and then after long hours of work day after day.）用以引起读者对下文的期待和阅读的兴趣。读者读到这里就想了解下面作者会说什么，为什么休息会对工作、学习有促进作用，怎么促进的。中心思想句为"An escape from worldly matters for relaxation to relieve the stress is a good idea for your mental health and for better work as well."（偶尔放松一下自己，给自己减压，不但有益身心健康，而且也能以更旺盛的精力干好工作，提高学习成绩。）"Driven by some kind of impulse of an escape from the endless lessons and homework, I decided to embark on a pleasure-seeking plan which resulted in the fact that I went to the beach with a group of my friends for a refresh last Sunday."为转折句，引出下面的正文部分。

第一自然段，即引言段交代了故事发生的时间last Sunday、地点the beach以及故事中的主要人物I 和a group of my friends。

Paragraph 2—3：

第二、三自然段为故事背景描写，即地点。第一句为本段的主题句，后面为本段主题句的支撑句，丰富场景的描写，不但交代了故事发生的地点，而且背景中还有人物，使背景活起来，一个游客如云的海边景点的画面在读者的大脑中浮现，这两个自然段构成第一个支撑段，烘托下面几段活动的叙述。

Paragraph 4：

第四自然段为过渡段（transition），用来引出作者本次出游的主要活动，即本文的故事。

Paragraphs 5—6：

第五、六两个自然段为过程叙述，从逻辑上可以合并为一个段落。本部分一气呵成，生动叙述了作者从接受潜水教学、潜水活动到水下见闻及感慨。

Paragraph 7：

第七自然段，即最后一段是结尾段，是对中心思想的升华。本段中，作者通过自身的经历讲述了海边出游后学习成绩有了很大的提高，重申（restate）了劳逸结合的重要性，对读者产生了有益的启发。

【范文1提纲解析】

Ⅰ. Introduction

A. Long-time engagement in work and possibility of a rest.

B. (Thesis) An escape from worldly matters for relaxation to relieve the stress is a good idea for your mental health and for better work as well.

Ⅱ. Body Paragraph 1 (Para. 2—3)

A. The beach, the air, the landscapes and the tourists.

B. Everybody was happy.

Ⅲ. Body Paragraph 2 (Para. 4)

A. Saw the sign of scuba diving.

B. Decided to have a try.

Ⅳ. Body Paragraph 3 (Para. 5—6)

A. Took some courses in scuba diving and got down the water.

B. The underwater world was wonderful.

Ⅴ. Conclusion

A. I did well in the exams.

B. (Restatement of the thesis) The beach trip helped a lot in my schoolwork.

【范文2】

Adventures in the Mountains

(1) Summer vacation came and we looked forward to a great time for play. No school, no homework. But our dreams were shattered soon by the fact that our teachers gave us a ton of homework to do during the vacation. Vexed as I was, I decided to stay with my grandparents in the country before I set about accomplishing those grand tasks. My grandmother cooked nice food for me on my arrival. As always it was to my liking. Most importantly, I had a great chance to play with my cousins, Tom and Jimmie, who were my uncle's children. We decided to go on an expedition to the mountains the next day.

(2) Day dawned with the crowing of the roosters. I grabbed a bite of the food Grandmother left for me before she went to work in the fields; then I started with my cousins amid the chorus of the mooing of the cattle, bleating of the sheep and grunting of the swines. The air smelt the odor of cattle, goats, chickens and all other livestock. We passed farm houses one by one along the narrow village street.

(3) Outside the village, we found ourselves on a way winding through the fields. We felt lost in an ocean of crops with rolling waves. Twigs were nodding gaily in the morning breeze, giving out fragrant fresh smell. Birds were chirping in the trees. At one point, we were startled by a big bird fluttering away from the trees abruptly, seemingly disturbed by our arrival. "A pheasant!" My little brother Jimmie cried excitedly and was ready to run after it. Tom stopped him and said, "Come on, boy. We have no time to lose."

(4) On approaching the mountain, there, a majestic mount loomed large and high in the thin haze, thrusting itself into the sky. I watched it in awe, admiring the creation of nature. "It is called Mount Goddess; few people dare to enter it. Old legend goes that whoever enters it will be eaten up by the monster who has lived

in there for many, many years," Said Tom, who was now playing the role of a tour guide.

（5）The way became narrower and rugged, parts of which washed away by torrents caused by the rains with piercing rocks here and there on the bare dried stream bottom. Half way up the mount, the rugged path broadened into something like a plateau and the plantations thickened. We could hear chirping of birds in the woods and rustling of some unknown small animals in the bushes. A squirrel scurried up a tree, nut in mouth, with a watchful glance at us, disappeared into the hole in the trunk. Jimmie ran to the tree to find the squirrel, but stopped suddenly, apparently frightened and, turning back to us and called, "It's a cave!"

（6）Coming near where the little boy stood, we were surprised by the sight of a dark hole in the bushes covered with rotten twigs and leaves. One step back, I picked a stone and threw it into the cave. The echo of the stone bouncing far inward lasted until it died away in the distance. Then all was still again. I came a little forward to the cave and shouted, "Hello, anybody there?" Ear-piercing echo of my voice came back. "Shall we go in to have a look? " said Tom. "Definitely a good idea!" agreed his brother. Plucking up my courage, I said, "I agree, maybe we will find some hidden treasures in there."

（7）So, after a brief discussion we made a big decision: That we should enter it and have a look. There began our adventurous cave exploration that we would never forget all our lives. Stick in one hand and mobilephone in another to light the way, we talked loudly and shouted to boost up our morale as we tottered on, stumbling now and then over rocks and corpses of small dead animals. Now we were taken aback by the sound of something flapping its wings and flying away over our heads in the darkness, sending chills down my spine and my hair stood on end. Jimmie collapsed to the damp floor and sat there, mumbling something to the effect that he wanted to go back. Gripped by horror, we sat down in the dust. Not to be beaten by horror as I always was, I rose to my feet and moved a few steps forward in the dim light of my mobilephone which was fast running out of battery. Stumbling over something, I tumbled down a pit. Luckily, it wasn't that deep, my two brothers came over and pulled me out of it. Another one-hundred-or-so meter inward we went, we saw a ray of light coming from somewhere in the distance. It was a narrow opening barely big enough for a child to go through. We went out one by one. The sun was still glaring so brilliantly in the sky that we covered our eyes. Letting out a long sigh of relief, we laughed at one another at the sight of our dirtied faces and hands.

（8）It was an experience we kept secret for ourselves for many years, for fear of being scolded by Grandma. We can still feel the excitement until today whenever we talk about it. When children today read ghost stories in the cozy chair and watch thriller movies online, I still cherish my childhood memories and my stay in the country with my brothers.

【点评】

本文以生动的语言、细腻的描述，记录了作者童年在乡下与堂兄弟们一起玩耍的趣事，讲述了几个少年的探险故事，故事情节跌宕起伏、惊心动魄、引人入胜，生动展现了童年时代的淘气、好奇心理与大胆探索精神。故事以时间为主轴，随着场景的转换，将读者引入一个又一个悬念，紧紧抓住读者的心，使读者有读下去的兴趣。

其中，第一自然段为引言段总起全文，提出全文的中心思想。第二至第七自然段为正文部分，叙述事件的过程。第八自然段为结尾段。

Paragraph 1：

本文的第一自然段为引言段。本段中作者交代了故事发生的时间（summer vacation）、地点（my grandmother's home）、人物（the writer, the cousins and Grandmother）。

本段的中心思想句为 "We decided to go on an expedition to the mountains the next day." （我们决定第二天去山里探险）。

Paragraph 2：

第二自然段为过渡段，以轻快清新而又幽默的笔触，白描了老家村子里清晨生机勃勃的生活情景，散发着浓厚的乡土气息。晨曦初现，邻居间鸡犬相闻、人们与大自然和谐相处。鸡犬牲畜、农家院落、乡间小街犹如电影画面一样，一幕幕展现在读者面前，烘托了几个少年出村探险的愉快心情。同时，本段也起着衔接作用，连接引言段与后面的故事过程讲述。

Paragraph 3：

叙述童年趣事，不妨来点小插曲，使故事更加生动真实，让读者感同身受，兴趣盎然，这种插曲就像在大餐中添加的佐料一样不会冲淡全文的主题，反而更能衬托出几个无知少年的单纯、天真烂漫，给后面的无畏探索做一个很好的铺垫。试想几个胆小的孩子怎么敢挑战黑咕隆咚的山洞？

Paragraph 4—6：

四、五、六自然段是主要故事过程讲述；冲突（conflict）出现在第五、第六自然段。"It's a cave!"一句标志着冲突的首次出现。英语记叙文要求有一个problem，故事情节就是解决这个问题。第六自然段描写了孩子们在发现山洞后是进还是不进的矛盾心理。恐惧与渴望探个究竟的矛盾心理跃然纸上，最终孩子们的好奇心占了上风，一致同意来一次人生难忘的探险。本段描写符合淘气小男孩的性格特征。

Paragraph 7：

本文的高潮（climax）出现在第七自然段。矛盾冲突达到不可调和即故事的高潮，是记叙文的显著特征之一。在讲述中，孩子们在开始山洞探险后险象环生，一只巨大的蝙蝠在头上飞过，在黑暗中令人毛骨悚然，几个小孩吓得面无人色，瘫坐在地，作者本人还失足掉进坑中。但是兄弟的友爱战胜恐惧，孩子们互相帮助，就此看到山洞另一头的一丝亮光，从而脱困。光亮象征着孩子们利用自己的勇敢和智慧战胜困难，走向光明的未来。至此，阿里巴巴式的探宝故事讲完了。

Paragraph 8：

第八自然段为结尾段。作者通过回顾、分享自己童年的趣事，引出对生活在当代的孩子们学习、娱乐的感慨，鼓励孩子们走出房间，放下手机，离开网游，走向大自然，培养热爱生活的情感。

【范文2提纲解析】

Ⅰ. Introduction

A. Background information

B. Most importantly, I had a great chance to play with my cousins, Tom and Jimmie, who were my uncle's children. We decided to go on an expedition to the mountains the next day. (Thesis statement)

    Ⅱ. Body Paragraph 1 (Para. 2)

    A. Description of village life in the early morning.

    B. We left the village.

    Ⅲ. Body Paragraph 2 (Para. 3)

    A. On the way to the mountains, we were happy.

    B. A little bit startled by some incidental surprise, the pheasant.

    Ⅳ. Body Paragraph 3 (Para. 4—7)

    A. Found the opening of a cave.

    B. Twists on whether to enter it.

    C. Adventurous exploration of the cave.

    D. Way out of the cave maze.

    Ⅴ. Conclusion

    A. Summary of the story.

    B. Comments and morals (Restatement of the thesis).

【范文3】

The Rescue

Everything had been totally different that Sunday morning, when the two boys had set out on their walk up the cool, pine-scented mountainside near the village where they lived. Near the top, Peter and Michael had climbed onto a rock to admire the view of the valley far below them.

> *The first paragraph provides the background information. Elements when, where, who appear in this part of the essay.*

That was when disaster had struck. On clambering down, Peter had tumbled awkwardly to the ground, his leg bent at a painful angle beneath him. Unable to move, he was forced to wait where he was, wrapped in Michael's jacket, while Michael had begun the long trek down the mountainside to fetch help.

> *Paragraph 2: What happened to one of the boys, Peter.*

Michael looked down on the mountainside from the window of the helicopter. He felt increasingly helpless, as it looked totally different from the air and the network of tiny paths was mostly obscured from view by the thick covering of pine trees. To make matters worse, the light was fading fast and a thick blanket of mist was starting to form. Eventually the pilot and the three mountain rescue workers in the helicopter agreed that they would have to go back and continue the search for Michael's friend, Peter, on foot.

> *Paragraph 3: The rescuers arrived, but with some difficulty.*

By seven o'clock that evening, they had left the helicopter in the village and gathered a mountain rescue team of fifteen men. Michael felt disheartened and scared for his friend's safety. Slowly they ascended the mountain, scouring the numerous paths for Peter. The only sounds were crunching footsteps and the crackle of static on the walkie-talkies that the rescue workers carried to talk to each other. The mountainside was an eerie place after nightfall and gradually Michael started to wonder whether they would ever find Peter at all.

> *Paragraph 4: The search continued.*

Suddenly Michael heard a voice come over one of the walkie-talkies, "We've got him. We're taking him down." "I'm sorry," said Michael to his friend later in the warm safety of the hospital room, "I didn't realise it would take so long."

> *Paragraph 5: Peter was found by the rescuers and sent to hospital.*

The doctors decided to keep Peter at the hospital for the night in case of complications with his leg. Before leaving, Michael looked down at his friend and patted his shoulder as, silently, they both vowed never to go walking in the mountains again.（来源于www.salor.org）

> *Concluding paragraph. Moral of the story: ...they both vowed never to go walking in the mountains again.*

【点评】

本文寥寥数笔对故事的背景（setting）进行了交代。本文第一自然段第一句 "Everything had been totally different that Sunday morning, when the two boys had set out on their walk up the cool, pine-scented mountainside near the village where they lived."设置了一个不错的悬念。结尾段…they both vowed never to go walking in the mountains again, 作者通过Michael 和Peter 的口婉转地表达了吸取教训，呼应了开篇第一句Everything had been totally different（since）that Sunday morning, 孩子们和读者们一起成长了。

本文开门见山，平铺直叙，没有明显的中心思想句，各段也没有主题句，甚至连个像样的引言段也没有，第一自然段直接开始叙事。这样的处理丝毫没有影响故事的叙述，反而使情节更加生动、紧凑，扣人心弦。写文章不应该一味地追求所谓成分的完整，有时候特定的故事特殊的叙述方法往往能达到更好的效果。本文的写作风格常见于小说中。

【范文4】

A Robbery I just knew I shouldn't have gone out that Friday afternoon. I'd had a strange feeling all morning, a feeling that something was going to happen, but I told myself, "Don't be afraid, Ida, you and your funny feelings! Pull yourself together and go and get the groceries." So I did, and you'll never guess what happened!	**Introductory paragraph** Ominous premonition permeates the paragraph arousing the interest of the reader, a perfect hook.
You know how someone feels when he is about to pay for his grocery shopping and finds his wallet is almost empty. Mumbling a poor excuse I headed for the bank, not prepared at all for what I was about to experience there.	**Body Paragraph 1** This serves as a transitional paragraph.
I was waiting patiently in the queue when suddenly two men pulling black masks over their heads, rushed through the front door and began shouting and waving guns in the air. "This is a robbery," yelled one of the masked men. "Do as we say and no one will get hurt!" The other bank robber herded us into a corner of the room and ordered us to lie face-down on the floor.	**Body Paragraph 2** A robbery happened.
I was terrified. My whole body froze in fear. Someone helped me down to the ground where all the other customers were huddled together, hardly even daring to breathe in case the men decided to carry out their threat and start shooting.	**Body Paragraph 3** We were frightened to death.

The cashiers were remarkably calm but I suppose their training had prepared them for such a situation. They busily emptied the contents of their tills into a bag the robbers had pushed over the counter to them. I kept expecting to hear the wailing of sirens as the police hurried to rescue us, but there was only an unbearable silence.	**Body Paragraph 4** The cashiers were calm in reaction to the robbery.
Almost as suddenly as they had entered, the masked raiders grabbed their bag and left the building, jumping into a beige getaway car. Minutes later, the police arrived. Several officers took off in their cars to see if they could catch the criminals, while others tried to calm us down enough so that they could take coherent statements. (Source: www.salor.org)	**Concluding paragraph** The robbers left and the policemen arrived.

【点评】

一个好故事的根本前提是故事本身的连贯性和生动性，没必要苛求要素的齐全。本文第一段中，作者营造了一个心烦意乱的氛围，整个段落中不祥的预感创设了一个不错的悬念，作者始终都没有写那个没有说出来的主题思想：今天要出事。结尾段既没有发表感慨也没有说教以便对读者起到教育意义，就是对事件进行一个直白的叙述，但完全不失为一篇优秀的故事。

【范文5】

Frustration at the Airport

（1）I had never been more anxious in my life. I had just spent the last three endless hours trying to get to the airport so that I could travel home. Now, as I watched the bus driver set my luggage on the airport sidewalk, I realized that my frustration had only just begun.

> 本段为引言段，其中I had never been more anxious in my life是一个不错的悬念。其中...I realize that my frustration had only just begun为中心思想句，主导全文。

（2）This was my first visit to the international terminal of the airport, and nothing was familiar. I could not make sense of any of the signs. Where was the check-in counter? Where should I take my luggage? I had no idea where the immigration line was. I began to panic. What time was it? Where was my plane? I had to find help because I could not be late!

本段为正文第一段：烘托了紧张的气氛，为故事中的后续危机做了铺垫。

（3）I tried to ask a passing businessman for help, but my words all came out wrong. He just scowled and walked away. What had happened? I had been in this country for a whole semester, and I could not even remember how to ask for directions. This was awful! Another bus arrived at the terminal, and the passengers came out carrying all sorts of luggage. Here was my chance! I could follow them to the right place, and I would not have to say a word.

本段为正文第二段：故事继续演绎，作者慌不择言，尴尬升级，直到第二辆巴士到来使情况暂时得到好转。

（4）I dragged my enormous suitcase behind me and followed the group. We finally reached the elevators. Oh, no! They all fit in it, but there was not enough room for me. I watched in despair as the elevator doors closed. I had no idea what to do next. I got on the elevator when it returned and gazed at all the buttons. Which one could it be? I pressed button 3. The elevator slowly climbed up to the third floor and jerked to a stop. A high, squeaking noise announced the opening of the doors, and I looked around timidly.

（5）Tears formed in my eyes as I saw the deserted lobby and realized that I would miss my plane. Just then an elderly airport employee shuffled around the corner. He saw that I was lost and asked if he could help. He gave me his handkerchief to dry my eyes as I related my predicament. He smiled kindly, and led me down a long hallway. We walked up some stairs, turned a corner, and, at last, there was customs! He led me past all the lines of people and pushed my luggage to the inspection counter.

第四、五自然段为正文第三段：情况更加糟糕了，关键时刻遇到了一位好心人帮忙。

（6）When I turned to thank him for all his help, he was gone. I will never know that kind man's name, but I will always remember his unexpected courtesy. He helped me when I needed it the most. I can only hope that one day I will be able to do the same for another traveler who is suffering through a terrible journey.

> 第六段为结尾段：不堪的开始，完美的结局，读者从中受到的教益是"爱需要传递下去"。

阅读与写作训练

一、拓展阅读

Please find the thesis statement of the following narrative essay and topic sentence of the supporting paragraphs.（试析下列记叙文的中心思想句以及各支撑段的主题句。）

1. Moments of Adrenaline

I was just listening to some music in my car as I rested waiting for my grandmother to finish up and we drive off. From the other side of the road, there were some kids playing football, and I did not give it much thought since they were just playing which is a regular activity. For a moment, I thought I heard the sound made by a hard-kicked ball followed by some noise from the children. I then decided to look through the window and see how far the ball was hit. Before I could even move an inch, another louder sound which shook my car came from the playing ground. That is when I felt fear all over my body and sweating profusely even though I was not sure enough about what just happened.

I slowly raised my head to check out what was going on. To my surprise, two boys who were of the same height were lying in a pool of blood. I realized that there was a black vehicle parked just behind my car and within a blink of an eye, the car run past me with the highest speed ever. I could not even gather my strength and my heart was beating so fast and I could hear the pumping sound.

A crowd had now started to gather around, but then I realized that my grandmother was nowhere to be found. My legs started shaking and some questions running through my mind. Is granny capable of murder? Was she taken by the bad guys? Is she so frightened to come out of the house? I collected myself and started walking slowly to the house. Before I could go far, I heard a voice calling out for me. And when I turned, it was my grandmother. We were both walking towards opposite direction.

I quickly turned and started walking towards her when the same vehicle that I had seen some few minutes ago came across the street still with a high speed. As they tried to drive away from the street not to cause accidents, they started driving towards my grandmother with a very high speed. I could not open my eyes and what was happening at the moment. I then heard a loud sound, and I now knew my granny was in trouble. Fortunately, the car had lost control but did not hit her. The car had hit a tree in one of the compounds.

All these activities were shaking me up. By the look of the car, the accident was fatal since they were over speeding and the car had been reduced to something that does not resemble any car. I reached for my grandmother and took her to my vehicle since she was also in shock and with her age, that was too much for her to take in. I could not feel comfortable just driving away and leaving the injured individuals. I went back and asked if there was anyone from the vehicle which was still alive. Only one had survived the accident, but unfortunately, his leg was stuck in between the seat. I, therefore, had to wait a bit longer as the strong men tried their best to save the man. It took us a couple of minutes to do that, and since no medical service had come to our rescue, I had to drive the victim to the hospital. I tried my best, but I could not stay on the steering wheel. I asked for help and all this time I am trembling and my heart racing. (Source: https://essaypro.com/)

2. Fireworks Show

The Fourth of July fireworks show at Fort Stevens proved to be a delightful outing with special friends.

The Barrett's first preparation for the outing was to invite their special friends, the Millers, to enjoy the fireworks with them. After the families agreed to meet at the fort, each Barrett family member began his own preparations for the outing.

One day before the outing, Mom started first with food preparations as she cooked potatoes for salad and prepared finger foods which insured light and healthy eating. Finally, the day of the event, she cut up bite-sized chunks of delicious summer fruits. The boys gathered frisbees, balls, hacky sacks, and other playthings.

Next, Dad pulled the cooler, lawn chairs, and blankets out of storage. Preparations were also underway in the Miller home as the mother fried tasty chicken, baked crusty French bread, and whipped up a delectable berry dessert. Both families loaded their cars with goodies expecting a great time of food and fellowship. When they reached the fort, the families walked close to a mile to reach their destination. Then they spread their blankets on the ground and set up lawn chairs around the perimeter. Then all around them, other families "staked claim to their territories" in order to secure a great view of the fireworks show. Next came the waiting for darkness to fall. Food and frolic filled these moments of fleeting daylight. The boys played hacky sack and catch until they lost a favorite ball in a nearby tree. Then, at long last, daylight waned and the fireworks show began. Background music being broadcast from a local radio station blared over hundreds of radios which had been brought by spectators. Then, choreographed to this background accompaniment, a spectacular display began. Sparkling, dazzling, creative combinations of explosions filled the night sky. So powerful were the fireworks, that the spectators felt the concussion of their explosions. Patriotic music rose above the explosive din. Then, with a stellar finale of a multitude of fireworks, the grand presentation ended.

Rapidly, all began to gather belongings in order to embark on the trek back to their vehicles. The evening spent with fellowship, food, and fireworks proved to be a memory which both families will treasure. (Source: Put That in Writing)

二、结构练习

Please write the outline for the following narrative.（请提取下列记叙文的提纲。）

Fishing Fun

Fishing at Horning's Hideout proved to be an enjoyable outing for Jeff and his family. All family members rose early in the morning excited to prepare for the trip. Mother packed food for the family as well as her books and needlework. Father checked the car to make certain it was ready for the drive. Then with Father's help, Jeff and his brother readied their fishing poles along with the books and toys which would entertain them on the hour's drive. When the family arrived at their destination, they stopped by the office to purchase some worms to use as bait.

Cheerfully walking along the narrow path, the family transported their gear all the way around the small pond looking for just the right place to cast their lines. In hopes that fish would be lurking in the shadows, Jeff and his brother decided to fish from a shady area along one side of the pond. Though it seemed like the perfect fishing spot, overhead branches interfered with casting.

Undaunted after snagging lines several times, the avid fishermen decided it would be best to move to the other side of the pond.

Here, the boys began to get bites. Before long, Jeff's older brother caught the first fish. Jeff caught one soon after. Suddenly the fish were biting and Father became very active helping the two excited boys keep their hooks baited, and reel in their catch. Just before noon, Jeff hooked what turned out to be the largest trout of the day which he hung in the water near the shore with the other captured fish. While Father and the boys fished, Mother enjoyed sitting at the picnic table and reading quietly or doing her needlework. After several hours of fishing, and a total catch of seven fish, Father showed the boys how to clean the fish before packing up for the trip home.

The outing was great fun for the whole family. Jeff and his brother found much excitement in catching the fish. Father enjoyed helping the boys and spending a day in the woods. Mother expressed her pleasure in being with her family and seeing everyone having an agreeable time. Most of all, everyone's taste buds were delighted with the dinner that evening. All the family is hoping for a return trip before too long. (Source: Put That in Writing)

三、写作练习

Ⅰ. **Guided Writing.**（手把手教写作。）

1. A Great Saturday

Last Saturday, I went to _____ .

First, I _____ . I also _____ .
Finally, I _____ .

It was a wonderful day.（三段式）

2. The Legend of Cape Luhuitou

Once upon a time, there was a <u>1</u>_____（猎人）who was <u>2</u>_____（勤劳勇敢）.

One day, he saw a deer when he was hunting again in the <u>3</u>_____（树林里）. He thought, "Hmmm, what a beautiful deer, but I must <u>4</u>_____（抓住）her because I need food." So, he went towards the deer. Seeing a stranger came near, the deer was scared and began to <u>5</u>_____（跑开）. The young man ran after the deer for a long time, until they came to a <u>6</u>_____（悬崖）. There, the deer stopped and turned her head; to his surprise, the young man saw that the deer <u>7</u>_____（变成）into a beautiful girl. They fell in love with each other and <u>8</u>_____（结为夫妻）.

<u>9</u>_____（从那以后）, the mount was called the Cape of Turning-back-deer, Cape Luhuitou.（三段式）

3. A Monster

Long, long ago, <u>1</u>_____（住着一个怪兽）in the mountains.

He was <u>2</u>_____（又丑又贪婪）. The people in the village were afraid of him but they could <u>3</u>_____（没办法）. This lasted many years and the villagers all hated him very much.

At that time, Monk Xuanzhang and his disciples were <u>4</u>_____（在……路上）to the West Heaven to fetch the Buddhist classics. Among them was Monkey King Sun Wukong.

When Monkey King <u>5</u>_____（听说这事）, he was so angry <u>6</u>_____（决心抓住）the monster and help the villagers. Then one day, the monster <u>7</u>_____（又来要美食和美女）. But he unlucky this time. He was <u>8</u>_____（打败并抓住）by Monkey King and became one of the disciples of Monk Xuanzhang. He was the famous character Zhubajie in the story *Journey to the West*.

So, the village was peaceful again and the people there 9＿＿＿（幸福地生活着）until today.（五段式）

Ⅱ. Write a narrative essay in five paragraphs using prompts given below.（用所给的写作范围写一篇记叙文。）

1. You went to one of the scenic spots near your home with your friends and you had a good time.

2. Your friend went to a wedding ceremony, please write about it.

四、思考题

Answer the following questions.（回答下列问题。）

1. How many parts are there in an essay?

2. What is a narrative essay?

3. What are the main elements in a narrative?

4. What is a hook?

5. What is the thesis statement? Where does it appear in an essay?

第三章　描写文

第一节　什么是描写文

描写文指的是用生动、形象的语言将事物呈现在读者的眼前。它可以记录一段见闻，也可以描绘人物肖像、山水风光、乡村田园、湖光山色或者城市风貌。作者通过生动逼真的描写，刺激读者的感官，调动其视觉、听觉、嗅觉、味觉和触觉，让读者如闻其声、如见其人、如临其境、如闻其香、如品其味。通过阅读描写文，读者似乎能看到画面的美感、闻到植物花朵的芳香、听到悦耳的声音或者品尝到美味佳肴。因此，把描写文比喻为作者是在用优美的文字作画一点也不为过。

描写文描绘景观、静止的外在形态和人物的情感变化、心理活动。这是描写文与记叙文的最大区别。记叙文讲述文中人物之间的关系、人物之间的互动（冲突）和人物之间的故事，主要写什么行为、产生了什么结果和怎么解决的，讲述其发生的过程。描写文只描绘景物、人物的表面和文中人物的内心活动，不讲述人物之间的互动和人物与环境之间的互动。

在人物刻画中，描写文主要描写人的心理活动，但又止于心理活动，记录人物的活动但又止于互动，不能有故事。描写文主要注重外观表象和探索内在，不讲述过程，不讨论因果，不提出教益。

描写文的主要定位就是描写一个物体、一个风景、一段见闻和一段经历等，泛泛而谈，不往深处挖掘，不具体到事，没有情节，不讲道理，不得出结论，不分析原因。描写文就是用笔当画笔超然地、泛泛地描绘一幅风景画或人物画。

在我国语文学科中不存在描写文这个文体，描写只是作为一种写作手法普遍存在于各种写作文体的创作中，尤其是在小说和记叙文中。但是在英语中，描写文作为一种文体而存在。

一、景物描写

Sample 1

Our house stands among some tall trees. To the east of it there is a plot of field grown with cabbages. A river runs gaily in front of our house and there are some trees behind our house. Far behind, it is a hill covered with all kinds of plantations that are green all the year round.

Sample 2

It was autumn, in the small hours of the morning. The moon had gone down, but the sun had not yet risen, and the sky appeared a sheet of darkling blue. Apart from night-prowlers, all was asleep. Old Chuan suddenly sat up in bed. He struck a match and lit the grease-covered oil lamp, which shed a ghostly light over the two rooms of the tea-house.（Source：Selected Stories of Lu Hsun By Lu Hsun)

Sample 3

The sun's bright yellow rays had gradually faded on the mud flat by the river. The leaves of the tallow trees beside the river were at last able to draw a parched breath, while a few striped mosquitoes danced, humming, beneath them. Less smoke was coming from the kitchen chimneys of the peasants' houses along the river, as women and children sprinkled water on the ground before their doors and brought out little tables and stools. You could tell it was time for the evening meal.（Source：Selected Stories of Lu Hsun By Lu Hsun)

Sample 4

The sun had withdrawn its last rays, and the darkling water was gradually cooling off. There was a clatter of bowls and chopsticks on the mud flat, and sweat stood our on the backs of the people there. Mrs. Sevenpounder had finished three bowls of rice when, happening to look up, she saw something that set her heart pounding. Through the tallow leaves, Mr. Chao's short plump figure could be seen approaching from the one-plank bridge. And he was wearing his long sapphire-blue cotton gown. (Source：Selected Stories of Lu Hsun By Lu Hsun)

Sample 5

It was late winter. As we drew near my former home the day became overcast and a cold wind blew into the cabin of our boat, while all one could see through the chinks in our bamboo awning were a few desolate villages, void of any sign of life, scattered far and near under the sombre yellow sky. I could not help feeling depressed. (Source：Selected Stories of Lu Hsun By Lu Hsun)

二、人物描写

Sample 6

... a golden moon suspended in a deep blue sky and beneath it the seashore, planted as far as the eye could see with jade-green watermelons, while in their midst a boy of eleven or twelve, wearing a silver necklet and grasping a steel pitchfork in his hand, was thrusting with all his might at a zha which dodged the blow and escaped between his legs. (Source：Selected Stories of Lu Hsun By Lu Hsun)

Sample 7

She had an oval shaped flawless face ... her skin was an olive smooth skin... her nose was a perfect shape slightly sloped upward ... she had a natural beauty...the kind you get without make up ... long lashes that even curled upward a bit ... her eyes were a light blue almost white blue and were so clear and looked as if they had a twinkle in them ... her eyebrows were a perfect arch shape. She had petite features, her ears were even small ... her face was small, she had perfect features like a models picture without all the garb of make up. Her natural beauty made you want to stare at akl her features and wonder which one made her so outstandingly in beauty ... her personality went along with her beauty ... natural ... herself, which radiated her beauty even more. Her smile made her look innocent ... when she smiled and shone her pearly white teeth the guys would stop and look on her beauty, her hair was a strawberry blond with blonde highlights which had a lustre shine ... framing a perfect feature face.

Sample 8

His white hair is thin and combed over from one ear to the other, if the wind blew just right it would stand up tall, waving like he was surrendering.

Dried sweat stains outlined each crease in his fat rolls, when he moves, there's a pungent odor of feta cheese.

The skin under his eyes has a yellowish tint, and the rest of his face has red spider veins.

Large pores clogged with filth speckle his nose, and bushy black hairs curled up the corners of his nostrils, matching the wiry strands poking out his ears.

His fingernails are thick and stained yellow from smoking for almost a century.

Sample 9

Everyone stared, she was perfect. Fresh-faced, petite with long blonde wavy hair shining as the sun glistened down. Christina was a naturally beauty, clear complexion with long, curled eye-lashes fluttering over her light-blue dreamy eyes. Christina wore a gorgeous shrimp-coloured skater-skirt tied at the waist with a think brown buckle belt, white cami-top and a gold necklace resting around her sweet-scented neck. Boys passing stared hopelessly at Christina knowing they wouldn't have a chance with a girl like her, however, little did they know she was going through a real tough patch in her life, she was torn between two loves of her life; Emmett and Dylan. In different ways she loved both of them and couldn't bare to disappoint either, she had many sleepless nights worrying about what were going to happen. They'd all been friends since they were little and she once wished upon a shooting star they'd stay friend forever and wished that they'd understand.

三、地点描写

The wine shops in Luchen are not like those in other parts of China. They all have a right-angled counter facing the street, where hot water is kept ready for warming wine. When men come off work at midday and in the evening they buy a bowl of wine; it cost four coppers twenty years ago, but now it costs ten. Standing beside the counter, they drink it warm, and relax. Another copper will buy a plate of salted bamboo shoots or peas flavoured with aniseed, to go with the wine; while for a dozen coppers you can buy a meat dish. But most of these customers belong to the short-coated class, few of whom can afford this. Only those in long gowns enter the adjacent room to order wine and dishes, and sit and drink at leisure. (Source：Selected Stories of Lu Hsun By Lu Hsun)

四、事物描写

It was dusk when we entered the tiny grocery store on the edge of the deserted road. The store was lit by a single bulb hanging near the entrance. The aisles in the store were narrow allowing only one shopper at a time. Ancient wooden shelves lining the aisles were cluttered with dust-covered cans and boxes. Yellowed labels on the cans held the secret of the store.

第二节　描写文的写作

前面已经说过在我国是没有描写文这一文体的，它主要是作为一种写作手法广泛应用于各种写作中。在英语中，描写也普遍应用于记叙文中，所以也有人将两种文体合并起来称为 narrative-descriptive（描写记叙文）。诚然，记叙文在讲述一个故事的时候，对故事背景和人物的刻画是离不开描写的。大段的描写可以烘托小说氛围，暗示人物心理活动和故事发展趋势，使叙事更具有画面感、真实感。

描写文通常是作者个人的游记或者记录别人的讲述或观看某画面后的客观记录。记叙文通常以时间或空间顺序组织安排故事情节的发展，而描写文主要以地点、场景的变化为主线展开创作。描写文刻画人物时注重肖像、语言、行为、心理活动及生活细节的描写，描绘景物时多以空间顺序的安排方式展开文章段落。

描写文标准的模式是"五段式"，初学者也可以使用"三段式"。创作之前，要收集素材、准备创作思路，撰写写作提纲，在提纲的基础上才能写出一篇优秀的描写文。

一、构思

将所有素材作一个整理，可以使用头脑风暴形式，也可以用图示导引法形成一个创作思路，英语叫mapping，如描写my house，可以作出下列思维草图。

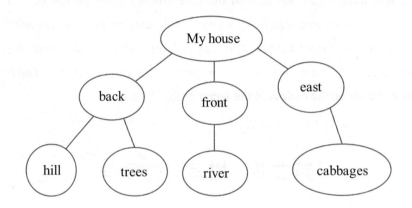

二、撰写提纲

描写文结构与其他文体没有差别，即引言段、正文、结尾段。描写文的提纲遵循"五段式"，初学者可以采用"三段式"。

在引言段中，作者交代背景信息。第一句要抓住读者的阅读兴趣，可以是引用别人对某人、某地、某物的评价或描述，也可以是自己的感言，如"East or west, home is the best."正文部分再具体地描写自己故乡的人文风貌、自然景观、风俗习惯等，一个段落描写一个侧面，不要涉及人物之间的冲突或人物与环境之间的互动，不然就写成记叙文了。

正文通常有三段，初学者也可以写一段。如果写的是"三段式"，支撑句要写至少三句。正文通常是全文花费笔墨最多的地方，如果"三段式"的文章写得十分冗长，不妨换一下行、分一分段。在实际操作中要灵活掌握，目的是方便读者的阅读，让读者一目了然。

结尾段呼应主题并结束全文，不拖泥带水，不提出新的观点，如不能说"我的家乡如此美丽，为什么不去那里欣赏旖旎的风光、体验浓厚的传统民俗？"在结尾段写提议、倡议、建议那是议论文的事。

根据不同的主题或者写作范围（prompt）自行确定主题后，按照上面所说的形式撰写提纲。

I. Introductory Paragraph	Introduction	A. Background information	The hook
		B. Thesis statement	Reasons why the author describes a certain object, person or situation.
II. Body Paragraph 1	The object being portrayed	A. Topic sentence	1. Reveal everything about the object, person or situation to be described. 2. Listing all the details which are important for making a vivid portrait. 3. Use metaphors and comparison.
		B. Supporting detail	
		C. Supporting detail	
III. Body Paragraph 2	The surroundings	A. Topic sentence	1. Show the reader all the surroundings of the described object, person or situation. The reader should feel like he is involved in the experience. 2. Use metaphors and comparison.
		B. Supporting detail	
		C. Supporting detail	
IV. Body Paragraph 3	Sensual and emotional description	A. Topic sentence	1. The writer uses his sense of taste, touch, smell, sound and sight to make the experience alive. 2. The writer needs to replay the object, the person or the situation to the reader. 3. Use metaphors and comparison.
		B. Supporting detail	
		C. Supporting detail	
V. Concluding Paragraph	Summary	A. General Statement	Restate the meaning and idea of this description in different words.
		B. Restatement of the thesis	

第三节 范文学习

【范文1】

（1）My favorite day is Sunday because it's a holiday for me.

（2）On Sunday, I like to wake up a bit late and will have my breakfast with my parents and younger brother. Then I will play football with my father inside our house. Sometimes he helps me in doing some interesting activities. By this time, my mother will cook my favorite dishes for me which I enjoy a lot. After lunch I will take a short nap with my family after a story from my mother. In the evening, I will watch some movies or my favorite cartoon. Evening my father will take us to a park nearby or any beach. Sometimes we visit our nearby temple. I love to play with my brother in the park and beaches. We will go to the market and buy vegetables and other items. On Sunday I will have my dinner on time and go to bed early so that I can go to school, next day on time.

（3）I will get more refreshed and energetic in my studies after each Sunday. Sunday will always be my favorite day.

【点评】

本文第一段只有一句，即为主题句或中心思想句（thesis statement），同时第一句也起着引言段的作用。第二段是正文，为中心思想句的支撑段。第三段有两句，是对全文的概括总结。全文流畅、紧凑、幼稚、清新，不失为一篇优秀的初级习作。

【范文2】

My Flat

（1）I live in a flat, with my husband and a friend from Canada. My flat is on the second floor.

（2）When you go in, you can find a hall. On the right, there is a kitchen. Opposite the entrance door, there is a sitting room and on the left there is a corridor to the bedrooms and the bathroom.

（3）The kitchen is small, but it's OK for us. In the kitchen, there is a window.

Its curtains are yellow. There is a cooker and a washing machine. Opposite there is a fridge and a sink. In the middle, there is a white table and two white chairs. Oh, there are some cupboards, too! for pots and pans, dishes, and so on.

(4) Next to the kitchen, there is a sitting-room and a dining-room. On the left, you can see the dining-room. There is a glass table and four black iron chairs. There is a piece of furniture with glasses and DVDs, and there are some pictures on the walls. On the right, you can find the sitting-room. It has a burgundy sofa and two green armchairs. Opposite the sofa is the TV set. I go to sleep in front of the TV after lunch! There are some plants and there is a big window. This room has a lot of light. I love it!

(5) The first room is my office. There is no bed. There isn't a bed. It has three bookcases and a lot of books. There is a desk and there is a personal computer on the desk. There is a printer, too. There is a CD player and a lot of music CDs. There are a lot of pictures — family photos and photos with friends.

(6) Next, on the left you can find P's office. P is my husband. He is a teacher. He loves reading, so he has a lot of books. He loves playing the guitar too — the Spanish guitar. There is also a computer.

(7) The third room is our bedroom. There is a double bed, an in-built closet, a long mirror, and two bedside tables with small lamps. There are no pictures on the wall. It's very simple.

(8) Opposite this bedroom, there is a bathroom. It doesn't have a window. It has no window and the walls are brown. I don't like this. So I use orange towels! There is a toilet, a wash-basin, a bath tub and a mirror. It's OK.

(9) At the end of this corridor you can go upstairs. There is an attic. It's very big and it has a lot of light. There are two single beds, for friends. There is a toilet, too. There is a computer and a music equipment. There are a lot of books and music CDs. Finally, there is a cupboard for the vacuum cleaner and for my painting equipment. I love painting!

(10) Finally, my neighbors are OK. They sometimes make a lot of noise, but they also help us.

【点评】

本文是一篇典型的描写文。从结构上看，本文有十段：第一段为引言段，第二至第九段为正文，第十段为结尾段。本文的thesis是my flat, 描写对象（object）是我的房子，所以只能写房子，不能在居住在里面的人和人的互动上花太多笔墨。

第一段首先告诉读者我的家在哪里、有几口人，同时告诉读者，下面的内容是介绍我的公寓。

第二段开门见山，从进门开始，进入客厅，开始介绍房子的总体布局，用以引领正文，起着起始段与正文的衔接作用。本段是一个不错的转折段。

第三段开始至第九段详细介绍了每个房间的位置和功能以及使用者是谁。作者用简单的笔触、朴素的语言清楚地描述了自己的家，犹如画了一幅各房间的图景；读者如身临其境，通过阅读本文对作者的家有了一个较为全面的了解，如同到过作者家里做客一样。

第十段是结尾段。本段呼应了第一段中本文的主题my flat, 介绍了我的邻居，丰富了本文的全景画面，但又没有浓墨重彩，而是一带而过，防止结尾句喧宾夺主，冲淡主题。

本文以空间位置的转换安排各段，由外及里、从大到小（客厅到各房间）、从左到右、从上到下，全文安排得错落有致，主次分明，逐一介绍了自己居住的房子。同时，本文在位置场景转换中大量运用了转换词与介词on the second floor, next to, opposite, on the left, on the right, 使描述更加具体准确，结构清楚、层次分明，是一篇值得初学者学习的优秀描写文。

【范文3】

The Librarian

（1）Over the years that I knew her, I gained an uncommon respect for the librarian at our high school. In one word she could be described as "eccentric", but only because she refused to accept the stereotypical notion of what the term "librarian" had come to mean. The students thought she was just plain weird, but those who took the time to know her realized she was a person searching for a comfortable identity.

（2）At first glance, she could indeed be a formidable figure to behold.

Her hair was most often in disarray simply as a result of her compulsion to go everywhere in tenth speed. Not only was her gait a marvel, but her purpose was also a wonder. She always gave one the impression she had a mission, and, at that express moment, had been called forth to duty. When classes would commence, she would proudly stride off to her room, as if a group of novice missionaries awaited her divine intervention.

(3) Her habit of dress, however, was not in the least missionary-like. In fact, the students used to kid her about getting a summer job as a highway flagman. The brighter the colors, the more she became entranced by their iridescence. As she flashed through the library, students became hushed as if a bolt of lightning had struck. In the morning, her emerald greens and hot pinks were eye-openers for the rest of us when she walked through the staff room door.

(4) Characteristically, her first words were a singsongy "Good Morning!" whereupon everyone would look up waiting for the next outpouring. She had an unconscionable taste for polysyllabic words — the more syllables the better. She used them with such flair, they looked good on her; and we could only smile, nod and try to make a witty rejoinder. Too often, we would be unfamiliar with the words, so she would again march off to another venue with the assurance that she had stymied the lot of us.

(5) Though she spoke precisely, as you might expect of one in her position, her voice was always at peak volume. A favourite response of the librarian's aide was, "You shrieked, madame?" In fact, students could audit her classes in the hallways, or on a clear day, even in the lunchroom.

(6) Similarly, her other ways did not resemble those of a librarian. She was easily flustered — not at all cool and composed like some of her predecessors. One particular day nearing the Christmas holiday, a very well-established physics teacher on staff kissed her full on the lips in front of almost all her colleagues. She went into a rage and made it clear that another such liberty would be inexcusable. Later that day, some mischievous students, who had gained access to the crawl space above the library, lowered a rubber chicken into her office, suspended a rope decorated with mistletoe. By the end of the day, her patience was severely tried and so it was no surprise to any of us when she polkaed too exuberantly at the staff party and knocked over the Christmas tree. What would have been embarrassing for many others was often summarily dealt with by "The Happy Booker", the pseudonym she was not unhappy to have bestowed upon her.

（7）When our colorful librarian moved away to a new lifestyle, a chic hairdo and trendy clothes, we felt cheated when a very acceptable, but normal lady came to take her place. Who would wake us up every morning with the word for the day? Whose voice would be ringing through the halls even after the last bell had rung? Would she realize she had taken a part of us away with her? Most importantly, would she realize the legacy she left behind?

【点评】

本文共有七段，其中第一段为引言段，第二段至第六段为正文，第七段是结尾段。

第一段中，"Over the years that I knew her, I gained an uncommon respect for the librarian at our high school.（中学时代最难忘最尊敬的就是我们的图书管理员）"为悬念句（hook）。中心思想句（thesis statement）是"The students thought she was just plain weird, but those who took the time to know her realized she was a person searching for a comfortable identity."

本文以时间顺序安排各段。作者用诙谐风趣的语言、生动活泼的风格，描写了一个性格古板、态度严肃、工作认真甚至刻板的学校图书管理员的形象。她生活朴素，不修边幅，似乎与这个世界格格不入，但对学生严中有爱、固执中不缺乏温情。随着时间的推移、场景的转换，作者勾勒出了一个似乎不食人间烟火但又充满人情味、十分和蔼可亲的校工形象。

结尾段以设问的形式总结了她在学校工作的岁月，表达了对这位老阿姨的不舍，呼应了主题，强化了读者对这位兢兢业业工作的图书管理员的印象。

本文刻画的是人物，但又不是静态的肖像画，而是一个有血有肉的人。作者在写作中对尺度把握得非常到位。描写主体如果是人很容易写成记叙文，作者拿捏得恰到好处，任何细节只写表面，点到为止，不往深处挖掘。

老阿姨形象栩栩如生，跃然纸上，但她没有"事"，即没有故事，本文没有安排情节。这就界定了本文是描写文而不是记叙文。本文使用了大量的形容词、副词等描写性词语，字里行间体现了孩童的童真、淘气与轻松愉快的生活气息，描写生动，扣人心弦，是一篇较为成功的描写文。

【范文4】

My Swimming Pool

As I gaze out my rear bedroom window I neglect to see the scenery all around my brown and beige swimming pool. I typically just think to myself, "Ah nothing different just the pool in the backyard." When the seasons change I don't observe the pool's altering environment. I think I'll now finally stop and admire some of the beauty and surroundings of my pool during the different seasons.

Paragraph 1: Lonely observation.

While I sit here and stare out my back window, I notice the immaculately tall trees shading the dock and pool. The trees seem as if they are endless. It is almost like they reach the clouds. Soon the leaves will change to beautiful shades of orange and red. Eventually they will fall and cover everything below it. The trees are also homes to many birds. In the early hours of the morning you can hear all of the crows cawing, and the cardinals chirping. When the weather gets cold I know personally I will not miss being woken up early by the sounds of the many birds.

Paragraph 2: Description of the trees, the dock and the pool.

Now even though the pool is closed for the winter, I know in my head the water is still crystal clear. For me I can see the bottom liner of the pool with the water, but there is actually a dark hunter green pool cover on top. The cover is held up by a big inflatable pillow, which floats in the middle of the water. All around the outside cover lays stagnant water. The water now holds as a good breeding ground for mosquitoes, or provides as a good drinking hole for my cat.

> *Paragraph 3: Description of the pool.*

As for the plants and grass surrounding the pool, they are still green and living. Even though, the weather has been extremely dry lately the grass still puts up a fight to keep from turning hard, crunchy, and brown. The plants adjacent to the pool have lost most of the frail white flower, but still have their six-inch long leaves. Soon the grass will turn brown and the leaves from the plants will fall, making the setting around the pool seem lifeless.

> *Paragraph 4: Description of the surroundings of the pool.*

【点评】

本文包含了描写文的基本要素，静态景物（object）、环境勾勒（surroundings）。作者从观察者的角度客观描写了窗外秋末乍寒的景象，生动地再现了盛夏过后的环境及树木，繁华不再，池水依旧，翠绿无复，往事如昨。通过描写作者婉转地表达了内心对季节变换的感怀，衬托了作者内心对人生无常的不甘而又无奈。但本文止于感怀，没有叙事。

作者在正文第一段中总述水池、树木及周边环境，正文第二段专注细节勾勒，周边景物、池水正中漂浮的遮阳棚，在读者脑海中呈现出来。

结尾段言犹未尽，作者寥寥数笔勾勒出了一幅总体环境的画面，以秋意渐浓的画面呼应段首中夏日里的最后一抹生机，并结束全文。全文的基调比较低沉、凄凉，但初秋写意还是很成功的，抒情遣怀效果也基本达到。

【范文5】

The Sunset		
Greg closed his eyes, leaning against the trunk of his old, favorite tree, breathing in the last of the long day. He lit up a cigarette and as he inhaled, the glow from the other end of it matched the sunset before him. Though autumn wasn't his favorite season, he had to admit there was something special about the autumn sunsets that nature had to show. He found himself watching the sunsets recently. The way things were going in his life, they had a calming effect on him and soothed his sanity which threatened to slip away from him with every passing day.	*The hook* *Depicting gloomy Greg* *Thesis statement*	*Introduction*

The season cast an orange haze above the horizon, lighting up the sky as if lit by fire, yet the haze was so crisp and clear. The sun, like a large, grandeur orange fireball in the distance was partially cloaked by the hanging clouds, which were all splashed with the random colors of hot pinks, reds and even hints of purples and blues. The sun was so large that he felt he could almost touch it. It seemed to look at him with a dull glare, knowing that its beauty and the planet's dependence on it for survival made up for it.	*Topic sentence* *The sun seems annoying.*	*Body Para. 1*
The sun which had its time to shine for the time it was given, seemed to whisper "Farewell" to the world as it sunk lower and lower in a lazy manner; almost as if it never wanted to leave. But Greg knew he too had to leave soon. He leaned off from the tree, walking down the grassy hill and ducking underneath the thick pine branches and towards the cabin. A cool breeze passed, making him stop in the middle of the field. He let the wind tossed his hair as it was almost like a human touch. It had been a while since he had been touched by another or even shook another's hand. There again, he hardly trusted anyone.	*Topic sentence* *Every dog has its day, human and sun.*	*Body Para. 2*
He looked at the sun again. The sun was almost as orange as the sky, like a ghost almost. Yet even from behind the trees, it seemed to stare at him; a silent ball of wonderment that was really a raging ball of Hellish fury. The very thing that gave warmth, life, light and happiness to so many could just as easily cause utter destruction. That fact reminded him of his father. Greg closed his eyes once more, the events of the day going through his mind like a reel. His father always told him to get out of the habit of daydreaming, but Greg was always the intellectual type. The "thinker". The sound of his father's words echoed in his mind, jerking him out of his fleeting thoughts. By the time he opened his eyes, the sun was gone, leaving behind a sea of dark, lonely clouds in a twilight sky. The heavens were beginning to litter the stars about, for it was their turn to shine.	*Topic sentence* *All daydreams will be disillusioned.*	*Body Para. 3*
He flicked his cigarette, brushing his nose while walking to the cabin. He knew that things, like the seasons would change and that everything would be alright. And like the sun, he knew everyone had their time to shine. And he knew it would someday be the same for him.	*All will be OK tomorrow morning, Greg and the sun. Concluding sentence*	*Conclusion*

【点评】

本文以第三人称的视角描写傍晚夕阳落山时分的寂寥以及主人公Greg的落寞心境。作者以细腻的笔触借景抒怀，借景喻人。夕阳可以无限好，人生得意，也可以象征残阳如血，昨日不再，失魂落魄的人在路上。一名优秀的作者要善于利用景物抒发感情，寓情于景，托物言志。本文中，作者使用了大量的描写性语言，以浓重的笔墨描绘了一幅秋意渐浓、凄凉孤寂的意境。此刻夕阳西下，天色将晚，又一个失意的一天即将逝去，主人公在这悲凉凄惨的黄昏怅然若失、孤独无助的情怀油然而生，感叹时光易逝，人生无常，犹如我国古代诗人曹操的名句"月明星稀，乌鹊南飞。绕树三匝，何枝可依？"

正文部分着重描写了Greg与如血残阳的互动，但是这种互动仅仅是主人公的心理活动。"Yet even from behind the trees, it seemed to stare at him; a silent ball of wonderment that was really a raging ball of Hellish fury. （夕阳透过树枝注视着他；它那巨大的火球就像寂静中的鬼蜮怒火）"一句中，即将逝去的残阳似乎是对他的嘲弄，又如挑战。此时，心灰意冷、垂头丧气的主人公那悲切的心境跃然纸上。

结尾段中，随着夕阳的逝去，主人公Greg恍然顿悟：原来人生也如太阳，有早晨的成长、中午的荣光和晚上的辉煌不再。人生都会碰到低谷、遭遇失意、承受失败与挫折，但这都是暂时的，明天太阳将依然升起，人生也将重新启航。文中斜阳落日似乎不甘而去，象征白日梦幻的破灭，但太阳明天依然会升起，暗示人生仍将继续，擦干眼泪明天梦想将继续启航。残阳不逝何来明日的朝阳？旧梦不去怎么追寻他日成功的荣光？

本文为一篇优秀的描写文，写人但主人公又没有"事"，只有以景咏志，没有叙述主人公遭遇到了什么事，不往深处挖掘。这一点作者把握得较为精准到位，值得我们学习。

阅读与写作训练

一、拓展阅读

Please find the thesis statement of the following descriptive essay and

topic sentence of the supporting paragraphs.（试析下列描写文的中心思想句以及各支撑段的主题句。）

1. My Neighbor

We live in a nuclear family. My father works in an IT firm and my mother is a teacher. I do not have any siblings nor do we have any relatives in the city. We visit my grandparents and cousins only during the summer vacation.

I felt quite lonely when we shifted here initially. However, I soon met Meera, my new neighbor. I was overjoyed to know that she was the same age as me. We were both eight at that time. I got along well with her from the very beginning. We connected very well and I started feeling really better. I was no longer lonely or sad.

Just like I became friends with Meera, my mother got along well with her mother. Meera's mother is a housewife. My mother and she often have evening tea together. We look forward to such days as it allows us to play at each other's place. We get a chance to play with different toys and games.

On other days, we go together to the park. We play different outdoor games, take swings and enjoy a lot. We also joined the same summer camp during our last vacation. The camp was for three hours daily during the weekdays. We indulged in many activities such as art and craft, dance, music and board games during this time.

Both of us enjoy art and craftwork. We prepared many craft items together even after we returned from the summer camp. During the vacations every year, we also visit the malls together. It has been three years since we have been neighbors and it has been a lot of fun.

I am really thankful to God for giving me such a good neighbor. Meera is simply the best. Her family is also very friendly. I am glad that our mothers are also friends with each other. (Source: https://www.indiacelebrating.com)

2. My Little Sister

I remember my 2.5-year-old little sister whenever I read the proverb "Action speaks louder than words." At this age, she hardly speaks sentences clearly but her actions speak instead. There are many lovely occasions which I remember and cherish while interacting with her.

I enjoy playing with her. Sometimes her actions make me laugh. She used to take our father's mobile, run towards me and point it to me. She will be very happy at that time. What she meant by this is that she wanted me to show her favorite cartoon — "Masha and the bear". Sometimes we will not hear anything from her. She will be so silent. And when we look for her, she might be doing something naughty like playing with my school stuffs or making drawings on the walls or making a mess of dresses in the cupboards. She is so happy when she gets chocolates or when we get ready to go out. Sometimes when we hear a sudden loud cry from her she will be crying in pain because she might have hit something or fallen down. She has a special sound of cry when she is hungry or sleepy.

I feel more attached to my little sister when my parents say her actions are the same as I did in my childhood. While playing with her, I feel my early childhood days are back... (Source: https://www.indiacelebrating.com)

3. From Baicaoyan Garden to Sanwei School

There was a huge garden at the back of my home, and it had been called Baicaoyuan Garden for generations. It was sold a long time ago together with the house as a package to a descendant of Zhu Wengong. Seven or eight years have passed since the last time I saw it.

In my recollection, it seems there were in fact some weeds inside, but for a certain period of time it was my paradise. Let's not mention the lush-green vegetable plot, the slippery-smooth water-well outer-wall, the towering honey-locust tree, and the purplish-red mulberry fruits. And let's also not talk about the chirping cicadas on foliage, the fat wasps on vegetable blooms, and the nimble skylarks lurking in lawn ready to zoom skyward all of a sudden. Just the surrounding area at the foot of the mud wall presented a lot of fun. Over there seemingly bell-ring crickets were singing in low key and grass-crickets were playing pianos. Had you turned over broken brick pieces lying around, sometimes you could find centipedes and blister-beetles underneath. If you pressed on the back of a blister-beetle, its rear orifice would let loose a spray of mist with a pop.

Vines of Fo-Ti plants and Mulian were entwined together. Mulian has similar fruits as those contained in water-lotus seed-pods. Fo-Ti has swollen roots. Some people said certain Fo-Ti had human-shaped roots and consuming one would transcend a person to a god. Therefore I always uprooted Fo-Ti plants and in the process ruined the mud-wall. But I had never seen one in human shape.

If you were not afraid of thorns, you could also pick raspberries which resembled ball-shaped clusters of tiny coral beads. No one would go into the tall grass because legend had it that there was a huge red-banded snake living inside this garden. Mamma Chang once told me a story. Long time ago a scholar was living inside an old temple while studying hard.

One evening while he was enjoying the breeze in the garden, all of a sudden he heard someone call his name. He saw the face of a beautiful girl on top of a wall who flashed him a smile and disappeared. He was thrilled. But an old monk who came over to chitchat at night spotted the hidden danger. He said his face showed signs of evil spirits'presence and for sure he ran into a "beauty-serpent". This monster with human's head and serpent's body would call a person by his name, and if he answered then it would come and chomp on his flesh at night. The scholar of course was almost frightened to death. But the old monk said it wouldn't matter and gave him a small box. He instructed him to put it beside his pillow, and then he could sleep through the night without a worry. Even though he did exactly what he was told, yet he couldn't sleep a wink and understandably why would he? Halfway into the night the monster came as expected with a rustling sound as if rain and wind struck outside the door. Just when he was trembling like a helpless calf under a hot iron, he heard a swoosh sound. Then a golden beam zipped out from the side of the pillow and afterwards it was complete silence outside. The golden beam also flew back and stayed in the box. The old monk later said the savior was a flying centipede which could suck out the brain plasma of the serpent. That was how it killed the beauty-serpent.

The moral of the story in conclusion is: if a strange voice calls your name, for goodness sake don't answer him. This story makes me wary of the hazards in life.

When I cool off outside on a summer night, I often get apprehensive and dare not look at the top of walls. Also I yearn for a box of flying centipede similar to the one from the old monk. That was always the way I think when I walked near the lawn of Hundred-Grass Garden. However, I never get such a thing I wish for, and I have never come across red-banded snake or beauty-serpent. Of course strange voices have often called my name but none of them came from a beauty-serpent. Winter''s Hundred-Grass Garden was relatively uninteresting, but once it snowed, things would be much different. Making snow self-imprints (i.e., making an imprint of your entire body on snow) and building snow Buddhas would require an audience to appreciate. Such activities were inappropriate because this was an off-the-beaten-track garden and visitors were few. (By Luxin, Translated by alex CWLin)

二、结构练习

Find the hook, thesis statement and restatement in the following descriptive essays if there is one and give a brief comment on how the body paragraphs support the thesis statement.（找出下列文章的悬念、中心思想句和呼应句，并简析正文部分各段是从哪些侧面支撑全文主题的。）

Food

Today, there are many delicious foods easily available. I sometimes wonder how life was in the ancient past when they did not have ease of access to food as we do today.

However, though I can find food of all kinds in our stores there are foods that stand out as my favorite.

I easily walk past the pizzas, the fluffy pasties, pies, and cream cakes. But when I sit in the restaurant and see the words oxtail stew, with creamed spinach and potatoes I positively drool.

The waitron places the crispy warm bread rolls beside me on a white plate. In front of me were yellow balls of butter. Next, she placed in front of me a bowl of creamed spinach, dark green finely cut with the white cream and steam coming from it advertising it was freshly cooked. I inhaled the warm aroma unique to spinach. Beside it was a bowl with smooth white mashed potato. Rich creamy smooth and firm from the butter and milk that had been beaten into it to add to its flavor and smooth texture.

Then came the bowl full of oxtail stew. Its rich dark brown color was set off by the white bowl it was in. The gravy was thick and rich. I could smell the aroma of beef, garlic, and herbs and spices drifting up from it into my nose. My mouth watered in anticipation.

Now I took the silver spoon and dipped it into the bowl of potato. It smoothly penetrated the firm fluffy white mound. I lifted the spoon and turned it over on my plate depositing a mound of potato. I repeated this 3 times. Then using another spoon I scooped up spinach dripping white sauce and put it on the plate beside the potato. The dark green Spinach was hot, the white Sauce melted and it contrasted with the creamy potato. Now after a second helping of spinach I took another larger spoon. I dipped it into the rich brown stew and stirred it. Then I scooped up a chunky slice of oxtail. Several other pieces followed that one onto my plate, the rich brown meat, contrasting with the dark green spinach and creamy white potato. The succulent meat gleaming with a coating of rich gravy and the aroma of gravy, garlic spinach and potato blending in the steam rising from my plate. I scooped up gravy from the bowl and trickled it over the white potato catching the scent of red wine. I broke the roll and spread butter on it and I was ready to eat.

Now the decision where to start, so I bit into the fresh crisp roll and tasted its warm soft texture and the melting butter. By then I had decided to sample the potato with gravy and the spinach. The potato was smooth, with a taste of butter over powered with the tangy gravy, its garlic and hint of good red wine in it. The spinach was a good foil. Smooth with its vegetable texture and plain white sauce it softened the taste of the gravy. Then I used my fork and removed the succulent meat from the bone. Its soft texture, fatty feeling in the mouth, the spice wine and garlic in the gravy made it perfect. So I sat contented at my table eating as much as I could, and more than I should of my favorite food. (Source: http://helpessay.xyz)

三、写作练习

Ⅰ. **Guided Writing.**（手把手教写作。）

1. Morning sun could be seen above the horizon and we were_____ on the sea. The red of the newborn sun cast its rays on the surface of the ocean and it looked like _____. It was my first voyage at sea and felt so excited. Our ship was _____ in the blue waves and there in the distance land _____. We were at last nearing our destination.

2. The airhostess was _____ with blonde hair. She wore blue suit and a blue hat, a typical _____. She _____ when passengers began to get on board the plane. She spoke in Chinese and English. She always wore a smile _____.

3. It was dark. I _____. I felt _____. I paced _____ in my room and didn't dare _____. I would be _____ at the sound even made by the wind or the meows of a cat. I was on the brink of _____.

4. Her boyfriend deserted her. She _____. Her _____ and she _____. She took up her phone and hesitating… and put it down on the settee at last.

5. The travel to _____ is unforgettable. The _____and the _____. What struck me most was _____ and _____. There were _____ and _____. I miss the days travelling there and I _____.

Ⅱ. **Put the following transitions in the appropriate blanks.**（选择合适的连接词填入下列文章的空格处。）

To sum up, Moreover, In fact, In addition, Consequently, Furthermore, Fortunately, However, Moreover, For example, In other words, As time goes by

The Weekend Market

Many tourists I have met have told me that one place they have to go is the weekend market. This market is huge and has everything from bags, souvenirs and handicrafts to many kinds of animals, many kinds of plants and it also has a variety of local food. 1_____, the weekend market is a great place for shopping and experiencing the local culture.

The market is located near the city's main bus station so people come from all over the country to buy and sell goods. 2_____, it is also near a sky train station and a subway station which makes it very convenient for city people, especially young people who don't have cars.

The market is very large and full of hundreds of small shops and stalls. 3_____, it can be confusing to get around. 4_____, if you get lost, it is a good idea to look for the clock tower which is right in the middle of the market. It will help you find your way. When I walk into the market early on a Sunday morning there are people and cars and motorcycles everywhere. You have to be careful where you walk. Many people are bringing their goods to sell in big bags on carts and trolleys. 5_____, you might even have to jump out of the sellers' way as they charge along the narrow walkways with their goods. 6_____ to the sellers, tourists and locals are pouring in looking for something to eat or ready to start shopping. 7_____, the market gets more and more crowded and you have to start squeezing past people to keep moving.

As you walk through the market you will experience many sensations. 8_____, there are many smells, scents and aromas. One moment you will be smelling the aromas of stir-fried cooking dishes from a small restaurant and the next you smell the scents of orchids and other flowers as you pass through the cooler and more relaxing garden section. 9_____, walking deeper into the market, your eyes will have trouble recording so many products with their many colors, designs and sizes. After a while you may feel dizzy and look for a quiet place to have a rest and a refreshing drink. 10_____, there are many small cafes and drink stalls selling fresh coconut juice, orange juice or iced water.

11_____, a day at the weekend market is both a day of shopping and a unique experience for your senses. It is a kind of magical journey that is great as a first experience for tourists and an escape from daily life for locals. 12_____ while it is usually hot and crowded, the atmosphere is friendly and good-natured.

Ⅲ. **Write a descriptive essay according to the following title or prompts. Before you do this write an outline for your essay.**（根据所给题目或范围写一篇描写文。）

1. My House/ My Flat

2. My Father/My Mother

3. My school/ My Class/ My Dormitory

4. Prompt: Describe one trip of yours to a beach, the mountain, a city, a farm or somewhere else.

四、思考题

1. What is a descriptive essay?

2. What are the differences between a descriptive and a narrative?

第四章 议论文

第一节 什么是议论文

　　议论文的写作目的是阐明作者的观点、意见和立场，作者通过缜密的思维、严密的逻辑论证说服读者认同自己的见解。为了实现这个目标，需要一个论点（argument），并援引旁证证明自己的观点是正确的，如事实案例、调查数据、科学报告、报章期刊文章、权威著作等。作者在写作议论文前要做大量的功课，包括通过网上检索、查阅书籍、实地调研、采访等方式搜集资料，尽可能详尽、翔实，资料要可靠，数据应当真实可查，不能凭空捏造。材料的来源越权威越有说服力，文章中引用的资料、数据、理论和语录要注明出处。如果是自己选题要选择自己的熟悉的话题，这样便于利用自己已有的知识和认识发挥与论证。话题不要太大，范围不能太广，论证可以旁征博引。一篇文章只论述一个话题。

　　议论文通常包括论点（argument）、论据（evidence）、反论（counter/opposing argument）等要素。与所有的文体一样，议论文通常有五段，但不限于五段，这是因为要想把一个论点说透彻往往需要从多方面、多角度论述，需要使用大量的事实、案例和数据等。议论文的主要写作手法是用事实进行论证、说理、推理，就是"摆事实讲道理"。一个段落结束或一个论证论述完毕，要有转场句导入下一个段落。写作中做好段落之间的衔接，让读者感到文章思维严密、推理衔接缜密，有较强的逻辑性，立意明确、说理清楚。论据的主次安排可以以文章的需要决定，一般情况下可以按照"次要→重要→最重要"这样的顺序进行论述。

　　通常情况下，先在正文第一、二两段充分论述自己的观点，证明自己观点见解是正确的。在论证正方观点时，每段支撑全文论点的某一个侧面，即为什么我的观点是对的（reason）。论证要充分，覆盖作者观点的各个方面，做到无可辩驳，让读者读后口服心服。同时，英语的议论文要求一定要提出反论。以"五段式"为例，正文前两段是正方观点，通常在第三段提出反方观点，先公正客观地介绍一下反方立场、观点，随后再进行反驳。语言要中性，立场保持客观公正，有理有据以理服人，不能嬉笑怒骂，冷嘲热讽。作者对反方观点超然、宽容的态度对读者来说其信服度是有加分因素的。反驳反方观点的主要目的就是要向读者证明反论没有依据，论点站不住脚，观点陈旧缺乏可信度，狭隘偏颇。

在英语写作理论与实践中，议论文有argumentative和persuasive两种。一般认为argumentative较为理性，以说理为主以理服人，以事实说服人，讲究实证引用科研成果，注重演绎推理。persuasive偏重感性，以情动人，不讲究实证。但是这种区分方法没有得到普遍认同，一般认为它们就是一回事，只是名字不同而已。事实上，所有的议论文都是在实证基础之上动之以情，晓之以理。对此我们不做区分。

由于议论文注重事实依据的特点，在写作时作者经常会用到举例、列举、原因—结果（cause-effect）和比较对照（contrast-compare）等写作手法。

第二节　议论文的写作

英语中议论文通常采用"五段式"。

引言段简要介绍论点及其背景，起着总领全文的作用。引言段结束时应该提出自己的观点、见解或立场作为中心思想，明确无误地告诉读者本文要具体论述什么。引言段的开篇很重要，要制造一个悬念（hook），抓住读者的阅读兴趣，所以开篇可以写一个社会关注度比较高的热点新闻事件、讲述一个故事、引用一句名人名言或具有一定哲理的谚语等。

正文段是论述的主体段落，所有的论据都将在正文中出现，作者以这些论据从自己的观点出发进行论证，从而证明引言段中提出的观点和见解是正确的。论据的主次顺序可以依文章的需要而安排，因文而异、因题而异、因作者而异。一般情况下，可以按照"次要→重要→最重要"这样的顺序组织段落进行论述。

　　结尾段简要总结全文并重申文章中已经得到证明的观点、立场及见解。议论文通常在最后一句中"行动倡议"（call to action），如So, let's not buy junk food any more. / Why not start studying hard right now?/ Therefore, don't use mobile-phones in class from now on等，它们类似电视上的"心动不如行动"等广告词。

　　议论文的创作首先要选题，然后收集材料、构思文章，在此基础上撰写提纲。

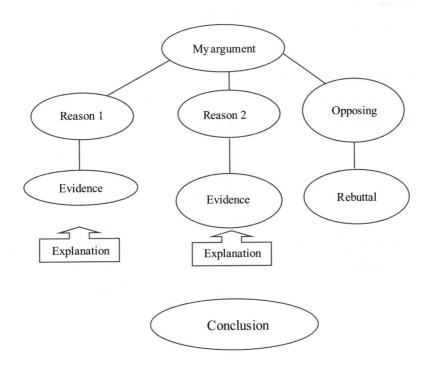

Outline of an Argumentative Essay:

Ⅰ. Introductory paragraph

A. Background information

B. Thesis statement (Your argument)

Ⅱ. Body Para. 1

A. Reason 1

B. Evidence

C. Explanation

Ⅲ. Body Para. 2

A. Reason 1

B. Evidence

C. Explanation

Ⅳ. Body Para. 4

A. Counter argument

B. Rebuttal

C. Explanation

Ⅴ. Conclusion

A. Restatement of the thesis

B. Call to Action

其中，reason是原因的意思，即为什么我的观点是正确的，它是每个段落的主题句。

初学写作议论文也可以采用"三段式"的格式，目前在我国大中学的写作中绝大部分议论文都是"三段式"。这种极简格式在论证较为复杂的论题时，就会显得力不从心，论证不充分、说理不彻底的弊端就会暴露出来。通常一个论据就需要一个段落来进行阐述，任何一个论题都需要从多方面论证、辩解或者批驳，所以需要重申的是"三段式"只能作为一个过渡性的练习模式，要写出一篇慷慨激昂的议论文必须掌握"五段式"。

第三节 范文学习

【范文1】

We Should Protect the Wild Animals

（1）Men as well as wild animals are part of the ecological system on earth. Over millions of years, we live on this planet peacefully together with not too much interference into territories of each other. But as technology develops, disappearance of forests due to aggressive human activities led to the extinction of many species of the animals when they lose their habitat. Absence of wild animals undermines the healthy ecosystem and has posed a big challenge to the existence of human beings.

（2）Diversity of flora and fauna on earth plays a key role in the sustenance of the healthy ecosystem on earth. The recent century witnessed an ever-faster-growing tendency that men are infringing on the living space of wild animals with the rapid development of modern technology, and it never stopped until today. According to one statistics done by the World Animal Protection (WAP), research has found 200 to 2,000 wild life extinctions occur every year with many more endangered. With the disappearance of wild animals the ecosystem may collapse and humans may face natural disasters and other survival crises.

（3）One reason why we are losing wild animals at such a fast speed today is that they have become a source of food for people in many parts of the world. This resulted in the successive outbreak of epidemic diseases such as bird flu, SARS, MERS and, COVID-19 that caused millions of deaths in the world. This has sounded the alarm for the whole mankind. We must stop eating the wild animals.

（4）Some people may say everything is ok without wild animals. Take the disappearance of wolves on the grassland in Xinjiang as example. The absence of wolves leads to too many hares who feed on the grass which in turn results in the shortage of grass for the sheep and cattle. In the nature, the fact that one preys on another is called the food chain. If this food chain breaks down, the whole ecosystem falls apart. This may result in the shortage of food and water for human beings.

（5）Existence of wildlife helps to sustain the healthy ecosystem. No man can live on the earth with the extinction of all species of wild animals. So, it's high time that we all took actions and start to contribute to the protection of wild animals.

【点评】

本文共五段，其中第一段为引言段，第五段为结论段；正文部分有三段，第二段和第三段为支撑论点，第四段为反论。

第一段首先介绍全文的背景，即人与野生动物的关系；第一句"Men as well as wild animals are part of the ecological system on earth." 为悬念（hook)，读了这一句关心动物的人士便会仔细地读下去。"Absence of wild animals undermines the healthy ecosystem and has posed a big challenge to the existence of human beings." 为中心思想句，是本文的论点即野生动物的灭绝将给人类的生存带来严重挑战。

第二自然段为正文第一段，引用了权威机构世界动物保护协会公布的数据证明随着科技的发展，人类活动频繁，侵占了野生动物的生存空间，导致大量野生动物物种的灭绝，这将严重破坏生态平衡，导致各种自然灾害频发，引发人类的生存危机。

第三自然段即正文第二段仍然是论点的支撑段。本段论述了人类多猎杀食用野生动物的陋习以及带来的严重后果，作者列举了多年来发生的各种传染病，如禽流感、中东呼吸综合征以及新冠肺炎。这些疾病给人类带来了巨大的灾难，严重威胁人类的生存。读者对这些灾难仍然记忆犹新，读到这里产生强烈的共鸣，对论点起到了极好的支持作用。

第四段是反论，以曾经发生在新疆大草原食物链遭到破坏后牛羊没有牧草的情况来证明反方观点是错误的。英语的议论文中一定要给反方意见留出空间，并将其证伪从而支持正方观点。

结尾段综述野生动物对生态系统的重要性，并倡议读者行动起来保护它们。

全文条理清楚，具有较强的逻辑性，援引了权威数据、事实等大量事实作为支撑，从正反两个方面对论点认证充分，具有较强的说服力，是一篇比较成功的议论文。

【范文1提纲解析】

Ⅰ. Introduction

A. Men and wild animals.

B. Disappearance of wild animals undermines the healthy ecosystem and has posed a big challenge to the existence of human beings.

Ⅱ. Reason 1

A. Diversity of flora and fauna on earth plays a key role in the sustenance of the healthy ecosystem on earth.

B. Human infringement on living space of the wild animals.

C. Statistics by WAP.

Ⅲ. Reason 2

A. One reason why we are losing wild animals at such a speed today is that they have become a source of food for people in many parts of the world.

B. Eating wild animals caused diseases.

C. SARS, MERS and COVID-19.

Ⅳ. Counter Argument and Refutation

A. Food chain breaking in Xingjiang.

B. Food and water shortage on earth.

Ⅴ. Conclusion

A. Both men and wildlife are part of the ecosystem.

B. So, it's high time that we all took action and start to contribute to the protection of wild animals.

【范文2】

Prompt（写作范围）: Nowadays more and more families send their children to colleges and universities with the improvement of their financial ability. In your opinion, what is the point of going to university? Write an argumentative essay expounding your viewpoint on the topic.

Why Should I Go to College?

（1）The answer to the question "Why should I go to college?" may be different in different times for different people. Many years ago, some regarded it as a way of changing their fate, others thought of it as a stepping stone of pushing their way up the social hierarchical ladder. Nowadays many more take it as a must-do for their kids no matter what they are going to do in the future.

（2）In the past, people from a poor family worked hard at school to get enrolled in a university because they wanted to change their fate while a better education background for children from a rich family might mean a further study abroad. All these would most possibly lead to a better future for them. Life in a city and chances of staying in a rich country were too tempting to refuse at that time.

（3）Today, things begin to change after forty years of rapid development. In ancient China, common Chinese people didn't enjoy equal rights of receiving education and their dream was to become someone who could read and write. Parents were proud when their kids had the chance to attend a school because they stopped being illiterate. But with the popularization of higher education, going to college has become a commonplace. Moreover, people may find a decent job with a fine pay even if they haven't attended a college. Going to university has become a choice and not an extravagant hope any more.

（4）Still, some parents stick to the old-fashioned idea that receiving higher education means higher rank and more wealth, which will bring honor to their family and ancestors. But this is not the case in the social and economical context today. Young people have a long way to go to become what they dream to be on graduating from the university because they have many, many yet to learn to become socially experienced and professionally skilled. The fact is that not all people even do what they learn at college. Going to college means a wider view to see the world and a door opened for more possibilities in life. In modern society, a university diploma serves as a stepping stone for the way of life you pursue, be it a white-collar clerk in a city or a farming entrepreneur in the country.

（5）We may be disappointed if we start with the conviction that we are sure to be somebody right after graduattion. Why shouldn't we start our career by trying our chances at whatever comes to hand and begin from nobody? We may also find we can be more successful in fields other than what we learned at college. Success comes from hard work.

【点评】

本文给出的写作范围是，随着老百姓生活水平的提高，越来越多的家庭选择送孩子上大学。请以此为主题自拟题目写一篇议论文。

这种只给范围（prompt）的作文，首先要做的就是要选择一个立场（take a position/stance）；有了立场后才能形成自己的观点（opinion/viewpoint），有了立场、观点之后就可以自拟写作文题（title）了，本文作者自拟的题目是"Why Should We Go to College?"

全文共有五段，是典型的"五段式"文章。第二和第三自然段是论点的支撑段，中规中矩，第三自然段是反论段。最后一段是结尾段，结束全文。

引言段第一句"The answer to the question 'Why should I go to college?' may be different in different times for different people."（为什么要上大学，对这个问题不同时期不同的人会有不同的回答。）是一句不错的悬念（hook），足以引起读者往下读的兴趣。本文的主题句是"Nowadays many more take it as a must-do for their kids no matter what they are going to do in the future."（今天很多人把上大学当成一种人生的"必修课"，将来做什么不重要。）

第二自然段（正文第一段）论述了从前上大学可以改变一个人的命运，追求远大前程。

第三自然段（正文第二段）论述了古代中国贫民家的孩子没有机会读书，但是现在即使不上大学只要勤劳也能找到一个高薪的工作，过上体面的生活。上大学已经成为一件寻常的事情，是一种选择而不再是不可企及的奢望。

第四自然段提出了反论，有些家长仍然认为上大学是为了光宗耀祖，升官发财，庇荫家族。作者从多方面论证了大学是人生的一个重要平台，在这里可以站得更高看得更远，接受过大学教育可以有更多的机会建功立业，会回报社会，生活蒸蒸日上。

结尾段总结前文，提出千里之行始于足下，毕业是事业的开端，实干是成功之母的理念。本段较好地呼应了中心思想。

【范文2提纲解析】

Ⅰ. Introduction	A. Why should I go to college?
	B. Nowadays many more take it as a must-do for their kids no matter what they are going to do in the future.
Ⅱ. Body Para. 1	A. To change one's fate
	B. To pursue a bright future
Ⅲ. Body Para. 2	A. To become literate
	B. To make more money
	C. For a decent life
Ⅳ. Body Para. 3	A. Old fashioned convictions on education
	B. More ways to be successful in a city or rural areas
Ⅴ. Conclusion	A. Doing what you learn at college is not always a good idea
	B. Restatement of the thesis

【范文3】

Prompt: People are using a lot of online language translation apps. Do the benefits of this outweigh the disadvantages?

On Translation Apps The importance and popularity of web-based language translation applications has grown over the past few years due to globalization. People from vastly different geographical zones, educational backgrounds and cultural beliefs are more inclined to use such mobile applications to learn and understand a foreign language. I strongly agree that its positives of this development outweigh the negatives, and, in this essay, I will discuss this using examples of current apps and The Times newspaper.	*Hook* *The thesis statement*	*Introduction*

On the one hand, there is ample evidence that constant access to mobile phones has been immeasurably beneficial to both our social life and business careers. Nowadays, citizens are migrating to different countries in order to build a new future and dealing with overseas companies for business purposes, so learning a second language has become their necessity. Such mobile applications are facilitating them by providing a handy solution to their language barriers. For example, Play store and Apple app store advertise multiplepaid and free to useapps such as Duolingo, Dictionary, Grammarly and Ginger which instantly translate one language into another allowing crucial communication, be it social or commercial to happen seamlessly. Therefore, it is apparentthat many key aspects of people's lives are being made easy through these handy and ready-to-use solutions.	*Topic sentence* *Closing sentence*	*Body Para.1*
On the other hand, whether language conversion apps benefit the public or cause potential losses to a key section of the education establishment, it is also a controversial topic for discussion. A recent study published in The Times newspaper has shown that there has been a significant reduction in demand for bilingual teachers or native language tutors as more people have started using such apps instead of spending money on the specialist tuition required to learn a new tongue. For an instance, free apps simply require basic registration details and email verification to register then begin, compared to the many hours or even years needed to master an additional language to a proficient level of fluency. As a result, despite the indisputable benefits of learning face to face, talented and experiencedprofessors, translators and interpreters are having to fight to justify their relevance in this new world.	*Topic sentence* *Closing sentence*	*Body Para.2*
To conclude, I believe that if the situation favours the relatively accurate, easily accessible use of online translation applications, which offer instant and quick solutions they can be hugelybeneficial for the community at large and in the future their flexibility and sophistication will continue to be improved. (Source: *An Essay Collection For TOEFL.* www. dethi. com)	*Summary* *Restatement*	*Conclusion*

【点评】

本文只给出了写作范围，要求作者自拟题目写一篇议论文谈一谈在线翻译应用程序的利弊。作者的选题是"On Translation Apps"，基本符合要求。全文共四段，除去引言段和结尾段之外，正反观点分别用了各一段论述。结尾段只用了一句话结束全段…and in the future their flexibility and sophistication will continue to be improved是对主题思想的升华。

【范文4】

I Feel at Home on the Duke Campus

When I visited the Duke campus last fall, I immediately felt at home.

The Gothic architecture and tree-shaded walks created an atmosphere of peaceful but serious reflection. The place is at once Southern—which, as an Alabamian, is important to me—and universal as it reflects the traditions of Europe and the classical world. The Trinity College liberal arts curriculum also reflects this unique pairing of the modern South and the global past. For example, I am considering a major in history, and am very interested in the combination of geographic and thematic areas of study offered by Duke's history program. The combinations of areas offer seeming endless areas of specialization. One interesting possibility is a focus in the geographic area of the U.S. and Canada, combined with a thematic study of Women and Gender or African Diaspora. By juxtaposing and intertwining these two foci, my understanding of the American South—and much more—would be greatly enriched. This innovative and flexible approach to both traditional and non-traditional subject matter is greatly appealing to me. I know by reputation and from a friend currently enrolled in Trinity College that the liberal arts curriculum is very challenging, but also rewarding. I believe I am more than prepared for these challenges, and that I will thrive in this climate.

Duke University's campus already feels like home; I believe that its academic opportunities will also provide a stimulating environment in which I feel I belong.

（免费资源）

【点评】

本文为"三段式"作文，短小精悍，遣词优美，逻辑性强，较好地表达了作者对Duke University的崇敬心情。段尾、段首相互照应，中间段落分层递进叙述，由校园、校舍到学习氛围，富有感染力，说服力强。

阅读与写作训练

一、拓展阅读

Please find the thesis statement of the following argumentative essay and topic sentence of the supporting paragraphs.（试析下列议论文的中心思想句以及各支撑段的主题句。）

1. Why Do People Go to a University

People study in college or university for many different reasons. I think the most important reason is to gain more knowledge and learn more skills. Of course, there are also many other reasons that people study in college such as to get more friends, and increase one's self-confidence.

These days, most jobs require people who are educated and have good job skills. Therefore, the people who want a good job have to study hard and at least graduate with a high education. Furthermore, as technology advances all over the world, more and more education is required of people.

Some people who study in college or university want to make more friends and increase their interpersonal skills. They enjoy their lives in university or college and tend to socialize a lot. They can meet more people who have the similar interests with themselves. They can go to uni ball after school and make more friends who they trust.

The people who graduate from college seem more confident in our community. These people are more respected by society. Many people want to be respected and to be important by family, friends, their bosses, and others in their lives. They find that most of them can confidently talk and do their jobs, as they are more educated. Therefore, most people want to get the confidence through the university or college study.

In today's society, people need more knowledge and skills to be adapted. The university and college study is a good way to achieve this. (Source: *An Essay Collection For TOEFL*. www .dethi .com)

2. Should Parents Let Their Kids Chat on Facebook?

Imagine a child as young as ten years old on the website Facebook chatting with a grown man or grown woman. Should parents let their children as young as ten years old be on Facebook? I think parents should not let their children or child be on Facebook because on Facebook there are a lot of things that are said and done that a child of that age should not be able to see.

If a parent approves of a child being on Facebook it is very inappropriate. Because that child may tell a story about their age and someone much older may see it and think their telling the truth and start sending them messages and the child might not like it at all.

When a child that young is on a website like Facebook they might get excited and go overboard. For example, the child might tell where they live, their address, and a lot more information that is not needed.

In conclusion I think parents should not let children under age get on Facebook because many different things can happen.

3. We Must Learn to Use the Internet

All students should be required to learn how to use the internet.

First, because the web gives students access to a tremendous amount of research from the comfort of school or home, they can save time doing research if they learn to use this resource. For example, if students want to write about poodles, they can easily go to a search engine and find all of the resources they could possibly want or need on the topic.

Next, the internet allows instant communication with access to everything from email to Skype. Students who have access to the web can communicate with parents and friends during breaks, resolving issues or letting parents know about a schedule change.

Finally, learning to use the internet will help students compete in the highly-competitive and technologically-savvy world. Many jobs today require employees to use the internet, and if students don't know how to do this, they will be stuck in lower-paying jobs.

Clearly, the internet is a necessity in today's world, so all students should learn how to use it.

二、结构练习

Find the thesis statement in the body paragraphs and write a brief comment on how the body paragraphs support the thesis statement.（找出下列议论文的中心思想句，并试析正文部分段落是怎样支撑中心思想句的。）

1. Prompt: Do you agree or disagree with the following statement? Parents are the best teachers. Use specific reasons and examples to support your answer.

Obviously, the first teachers we have in our lives in most cases are our parents. They teach us to walk, to speak, and to have good manners before we reach "the real world". More than even the professional teachers that we have in school, parents are generally the most involved in the development and education of children.

Almost for sure our parents are the best teachers at the beginning of our lives, which actually corresponds to the parents' role in nature. Parents are most committed and involved in teaching their children; they have a kind of instinct to sacrifice a part of themselves for the betterment of their children. They love us and have great patience while passing down their knowledge to us. They wish us a success and thus will not teach us bad things. And of course, implicit learning occurs when children unconsciously copy some of their parents' habits and styles of behavior.

During the second stage of child development, adolescence, parents can still be in the best position to offer advice even though the children might not accept it. In this case, perhaps the child's friends would be the best teachers. Adolescents are notoriously rebellious in many cultures and may automatically reject any advice from their parents. My first marriage for instance, was solely a matter of doing the opposite when my parents tried to intrude in offering their advice. So in such matters, parents should be much more flexible and be rather the partners with their children. So we can see that being a teacher of growing child become more and more complicated case as the time passes and many parents are simply not able to meet the increased demands.

On the other hand, I would say that parents are not professional teachers and they tend to be very biased by their love of their children. So wishing good things and an easy life may prevent children from maturation. In any case, parents usually can present only one viewpoint of the world, while good teaching should be based on different attitudes. Thus, when children go to school and have a great diversity of teachers, they learn much more than their parents could probably give them. Furthermore, once our parents get older, they become more conservative and cannot always be objective in regard to modern trends and fashions. Thus we need to take their advice with caution during that period. However, some kind of intuition, which I believe, shared between relatives about what everybody needs and great love, which exists in families, still makes our parents very good teachers and advisers at any time.

In conclusion, while parents are not the ideal teachers, and well-rounded children will generally need a great diversity of teachers in their lives in order to have a more accurate view of the world, parents are generally the most committed of all teachers and have the greatest emotional investment in their children and their future. (Source: *An Essay Collection for TOEFl*. www.dethi.com)

2. Prompt: It has been said, "Not everything that is learned is contained in books." Compare and contrast knowledge gained from experience with knowledge gained from books. In your opinion, which source is more important? Why?

People always are learning and practicing through their whole lives. From reading words in textbook such as toy, car, train etc., people have the concept and ideas. They further understand the actual meaning of these words by playing toys and riding or driving cars, trains etc.

Education (books) and experience are the main two channels for People to gain their knowledge. Each plays different roles for people. In my opinion, knowledge from experience is more important than that from books.

Experience first can prove if the knowledge from books are true or false. Textbooks are very wonderful in teaching people essential principles, how is the world looks like? What is the basic law of change of people and things? We can learn a lot through primary school, secondary school until university. However, people can only understand the really meaning of those form books and justify them if they are right through practices. A few hundred years ago, people learnt from textbook that the earth was flat. However scientists found that was wrong through observations and measurement.

The knowledge from experience can improve and advance The world and our society. As books have limitation, they only teach us what people found in the past. The knowledge from the books are constrained to the certain conditions and environment. For example, mould and tools design for plastics industry, the university course only taught me very simple cases, most knowledge is obtained from various different and complicated cases in my career.

There are a lot new inventions and new products, which could not be found from textbooks. Our society and world are developed through continuous practices, those knowledge, never found in books, such as internet, e-business etc. are all developed through new practices.

"The truth comes from practices and experience", people are continually discovering new things and assessing the creditability of the knowledge written in books. The knowledge from experience helps us much more than those from books. (Source: *An Essay Collection for TOEFl.* www.dethi.com)

3. Prompt: "When people succeed, it is because of hard work. Luck has nothing to do with success." Do you agree or disagree with the quotation above? Use specific reasons and examples to explain your position.

I fully agree with the claim that there is no correlation between success and luck. Moreover, I understand success to refer to one's ability to achieve the predominant part of his goals in his lifetime, which in turn leads to a correlation between success and income since the accomplishment of such a natural goal as to provide a good future for your loved ones demands the means. What is the simplest and most lawful way to earn enough to consider you a successful person? To receive a good education and to find a good job. Both receiving an education and making a career presuppose one's readiness to work hard, and success without hard work is simply not possible for the vast majority of the world's population. The reasons and examples listed below will strengthen my point of view.

First of all, considering an education and a career as key factors of success, one will choose to pursue a degree from a college or a university. One wishing to be admitted to the university will have to take several tests. It is doubtful that someone will be so lucky that knowing nothing; he could pass the test with a high score. A low score means failure, and that test taker will not likely be admitted. Therefore, in order to be successful, one should prepare for the tests and work hard, because a good education will provide him with a good job and an opportunity to accomplish some of his goals and dreams. In my lifetime, I have never met a person who could graduate from a college without working hard.

Secondly, it is impossible to make a career if one is indolent and lacking knowledge, at least in developed countries. Luck plays no role in achieving this success. Even if someone was unbelievably lucky enough to become a manager not being qualified enough, he will be asked to resign in the near future because of his inability due to lack of knowledge and experience to make right decisions. For instance, I used to work for a very small company owned by a friend. This company was later closed because of bankruptcy. The cause of bankruptcy was wrong strategies and decisions made by the owner. After the failure, he went to a university and worked for another company so that he could obtain experience and become a successful businessman. Nowadays, he considers himself a successful person because he had turned into reality his two biggest dreams of producing consumer goods of high quality and making charitable donations to needy people.

In sum, as long as someone understands success as an ability to turn into reality some of his dreams and goals, he will have to work hard because he will need money. And his chances to earn that money will remarkably increase if he could graduate from a college and make a career. All of these things are simply not possible without hard work. Luck has no place in such a scheme of events. (Source: *An Essay Collection for TOEFl*. www.dethi.com)

三、写作练习

Ⅰ. **Guided Writing.**（手把手教写作。）

1. I like_____. First, _____. Second, _____. Last, _____. _____ is really my favorite.

2. The reason why I _____ is because _____. Firstly, _____. Next, _____. Last but not least, _____. What about you?

3. There are many reasons for being a good reader. One important reason to be a good reader is _____. Another important reason to become a good reader is _____. This is important because _____, Being a good reader takes time but it is worth it.

4. I hate being told to do this and that. First, _____. Second, _____. Next, _____. Furthermore, _____.

5. People say that water is _____.

We _____. In our life,_____. We use water_____.

Sometimes , we_____.

But everything has two sides. Water also has the bad sides, _____. What's more, _____. At last, _____.

So, let's _____.

6. With the development of our society, people's lifestyle change from day to day. It has become more common for people to have different part-time jobs. _____. For some people, part-time jobs _____.

The most important advantage of part-time jobs is that _____.

Part-time jobs also offer people a chance to _____.

However, _____.

We may have to think about what we are pursuing in our lives before we bury into the work. Time lost will not come back. It is high time that we balanced family, schoolwork and part-time jobs.

Ⅱ. Write an essay using prompts given below. (用所给写作范围要求写作文。**)**

1. You chat on the Wechat day and night and it consumes a lot of time and energy. Please write an argumentative essay on whether or not we should be online all the time.

2. Somebody hates to obey the traffic rules and died in an accident some time ago. Please write anessay on this topic.

3. Dogs are man's good friends, but many people don't like them for many reasons. Provide youropinions and evidence to persuade your reader.

4. Please elaborate on both sides of online education which you experienced during the covid-19 virus outbreak.

5. Wives are supposed to take care of the family and do all the housework while the husbands take it for granted to enjoy themselves whether they are engaged in work or not, which is still the common practice in many parts of the world today. Do you agree or disagree with this?

第五章　说明文

第一节　什么是说明文

  对人和事物进行描述、介绍以及对某事的操作步骤进行说明的文章就是说明文。说明文是一种常用文体，在生产、生活和科学报告中有着广泛的应用，其主要作用是描述人和事物、揭示事物的内在规律和联系、解释各种现象的原理和说明事物的真相。说明文要采用中性客观的视角，通常以第三人称来写，不能掺杂作者的个人感情，不提出观点、建议，就是对一个事物的客观介绍和说明，让读者读过后明白事情的来龙去脉、前因后果、前世今生。由于说明文的这些特点，用户指南、使用说明和操作规程通常都是典型的说明文。说明文的行文应该是规范正式的，语言必须是标准的，不可使用方言、俚语，以确保任何地区的人都能看懂。

  说明文的主要功能是说明、告知、描述、阐述与解释，因此它必须包含有用的信息。说明文的写作中不提出建议、意见和观点，没有感情色彩，这也是说明文与描写文的主要区别。首先，描写文在描写事物、景观的时候作者可以表达自己的好恶，也可以赞美和感叹，而说明文仅仅是客观的描述。其次，说明文与议论文一样用到了数据、事例，用以证实和推论，这些特征与议论文颇有些相似。它们之间的区别是议论文的作者持有立场，即支持一种观点，反驳另一种观点，同时议论文的结尾还有行动倡议（call to action），而这些说明文是不能有的。例如：

【说明文】

  The new make cellphone of Huawei is $12.18 \times 6.858 \times 0.99$ cm in size, light in weight. It is of three colors, red, black and golden with cool design and functions updated.

【描写文】

The new make cellphone of Huawei is $12.18 \times 6.858 \times 0.99$ cm in size, light in weight. It is of three colors, red, black and golden with cool design and functions updated. <u>I like the one in red, it's cool!</u>

【议论文】

The new make cellphone of Huawei is $12.18 \times 6.858 \times 0.99$ cm in size, light in weight. It is of three colors red, black and golden with cool design and functions updated. <u>I prefer Huawei cellphones to iPhones because it is designed and manufactured by Chinese and I strongly recommend you become Huawei users, too.</u>

【广告】

The new make cellphone of Huawei is $12.18 \times 6.858 \times 0.99$ cm in size, light in weight. It is of three colors, red, black and golden with cool design and functions updated. <u>It will be on sale next month. You may buy one in any of our franchised shops in city.</u>

由于说明文需要描写（describe）、解释（explain）、说明（expose）、揭示（expound）和阐述（clarify）事物的真相和道理，避免不了需要用事实、数据、事例等材料，给读者一个正确无误的描述。因此，在写作中常用有举例、列举、对比—对照、原因—结果等写作手法。同时，在说明文写作时应该做足调研、查阅大量资料，确保文章向读者提供正确无误的数据、实事和案例，写作态度要严谨，逻辑要缜密，过程解释要清楚，步骤要具体，必要时需要有图示说明。说明文要经得住推敲和科学验证。

从写作目的上看，说明文可以划分为描写型、过程描述型、对比—对照型、原因—结果型、解决问题型和概念定义型六种类型。个人简历、城市介绍、导游词、解说词、产品操作手册、广告和调研报告等都属于说明文。科研论文写作（academic writing）有专门的格式，我们这里不涉及。

第二节 说明文的写作

说明文的格式通常采用"五段式",有些操作流程的说明(how-to essays)一个步骤可以一段,其全文可能远远超过五段。

一般情况下说明文按照工作流程先后顺序写作即可。自拟题目的时候需要注意的是,选择题目的范围不要太大,要选择自己熟悉的具体事物来说明、解释,如果范围太广超出自己的认知,不但难以掌控其长度,而且还可能导致错误的描写与解释。

开始写作前要做一些必需的调查研究,需要的时候还应该请教他人。然后就要开始酝酿、构思,就是我们前几章里说的头脑风暴。下面以介绍小动物为例简要说明。

Prompt: Choose a small animal and write an expository essay about it.

The Bat

根据以上的写作提示,选择文题"The Bat"。蝙蝠自古以来就不是一个受到人类待见的小动物,东西方的传说中都赋予了这种小动物许多不好的联想和寓意。在写作之前可以进行brainstorming。头脑风暴有两种方法,其中一种是段落部分学过的free writing,还有一种就是mapping或者叫 concept map,就是联想图,很像现在流行的思维导图。

1. Free Writing

2. Mapping

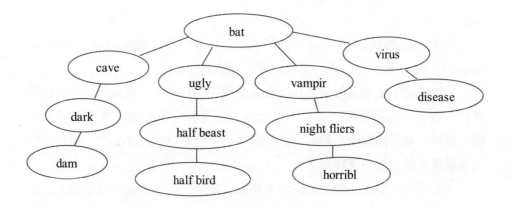

3. 在此基础之上列出写作提纲。

(1) Outline (5-paragraph Format)

Ⅰ. Introduction

A. Bats are the only flying mammals that inhabit in damp caves and may be found in most parts of the world.

B. There are many misunderstandings about bats and still they are considered dangerous creatures.

Ⅱ. Body Para. 1

A. Ugly, half beast half bird

B. Black or brown wings without fur

C. Avoid the sunshine and stay near water

Ⅲ. Body Para. 2

A. Live in dark damp caves far from human community

B. Feed on insects and pets

C. Detail

D. Come out for food only at night

E. Legends about them

F. Misunderstandings

Ⅳ. Body Para. 3

A. Carrier of over one thousand viruses

B. Cause diseases, SARS, Mers and COVID-19

C. Detail

V. Conclusion

A. One of the creatures that contribute to the diversity of the world

B.Stay away from the bats and protect the wild animals

(2) Outline (3-paragraph Format)

The Bats

Ⅰ. Introduction	A. Background information about bats
	B. Thesis statement
Ⅱ. Body	A. Appearance
	B. Distribution
	C. Habits
	D. Legends
	E. Viruses
Ⅲ. Conclusion	A. Misunderstandings about bats
	B. Keep off bats

第三节　范文学习

【范文1】

The Bat

（1）Bats can be found on almost every continent of the earth. They are half-beast-and-half-bird creatures who mostly live in caves. They have been misunderstood by humans for thousands of years and were given unfair associations with darkness, death and evils. As time goes on, human beings come to know them better and begin to look at them in a more objective way.

(2) Bats are the only mammals capable of flights, but exposure of their naked wings to the sun may cause loss of water, so they come out only at nights and their roost caves must be near the water. Nocturnal flights also help them avoid predators and it's easier to catch their prey when they are sleeping.

(3) Bats are usually black or brown in color with hog-nosed faces. They were given associations to evils and bad luck from a long time ago in different cultures. In many myths and folklores they were blood-sucking vampires. The reason why bats are so misunderstood by man may be that they are nocturnal creatures. They come out only at nights and are unfamiliar and mysterious to people. Another reason for this misconception may be that they are considered ugly by many people.

(4) Bats live in groups in caves and there are more than 1,200 species who populate in every part of the world except the arctic areas. They cling to the rock and hang from the ceilings when they rest. They go out for food on their night flights. They can navigate at night by using a system of echolocation.

(5) Bats are very important to human beings in agriculture for their predation on insect pests and they also help a lot in pollination and seed dispersal. One bat can eat between 600 and 1,000 mosquitoes and other insect pests in just one hour.

(6) Researchers have found bats are carriers of over one thousand viruses and bacteria and may transmit rabies to other mammals like cattle and other livestock, they seldom appear in human's life like what is told in myths and folklores. Allegedly, they were the source of the viruses that caused outbreaks of SARS in 2006 and Covid-19 in 2020.

(7) Bats are of vital importance in maintaining a healthy ecosystem and they contribute to the diversity of wildlife on earth.

References:

1. Don E. WilsonBat [EB/OL]. (Feb. 12, 2020). https://www.britannica.com/animal/bat-mammal#accordion-article-history;

2. EditorBat[EB/OL]. https://symbolism.fandom.com/wiki/Bat;

3. Factmonster EditorBats [EB/OL].（Feb. 21, 2017）. https://www.factmonster.com/bats；

4. Editor BATS - MYTHS, FOLKLORE AND FACTS [EB/OL]. http://www.crystalwind.ca/mystical-magical/legends-fables-and-lore/folklore/bats-myths-folklore-and-facts.

【点评】

本篇范文共七段，其中第一段为引言段，第二至六段为正文部分，第七段为结尾段。全文引用了大量的资料，以科学、客观的态度全面翔实地介绍了蝙蝠的前世今生，全文没有一句评论的语句，立场客观超然，是一篇典型的说明文。本文以上述的提纲写就，读者可以对照提纲进行学习。

引言段提供了蝙蝠的相关背景知识，提出了本文的中心思想句："As time goes on, human beings come to know them better and begin to look at them in a more objective way."中心思想句总领全文，对正文部分起到了规定和提携的作用。

第二自然段开始是正文。正文诸段落也叫中心思想的支撑段。正文部分有五段，从蝙蝠的外表、生活习性、分布区域、对人类的重要性、民间传说、人类对它们的误解以及它们身上携带的病毒几个方面介绍了蝙蝠这个物种。正文部分从各个方面对全文的主题进行了支撑和说明，使读者在阅读完此文后对蝙蝠有了一个较为全面的了解，能够以更加客观公正、科学的态度看待这种野生生物。

最后一段是结尾段。说明文的结尾段仍然要以客观超然的态度来总结全文，呼应主题，立场不偏不倚。需要注意的是，说明文的结尾一不小心就容易写成议论文。所以，我们在写结尾段时不能感叹，不能发感慨，也不要写call to action（行动倡议）。

本文的最后列出了references。由于蝙蝠是一种不常见的野生动物，与人类的交集不多，我们对它们的了解非常有限，因此作者在创作本文的时候需要上网查阅大量的资料。这些资料必须以参考书目的形式列在文章的最后，英语叫reference list或bibliography，它们的区别是bibliography是参考过的资料，而reference则是文中引用过的资料。同时，reference也可以放在圆括号内出现在被引用资料的后面，叫作in-text reference或in-text citation（文内引用）。

引用、参考了其他资料或作者的文章，一定要在文章的最后列出，否则会被视作剽窃行为（plagiarism），情况严重时会受到原作者的起诉，承担法律责任。所以，我们在初学的时候就要养成不抄袭、不剽窃的好习惯。人不是万能的，不可能什么都知道，参考、引用别人的作品不是一件丢脸的事情，但令人尴尬的是不尊重原作者的劳动而受到指责甚至导致其他严重后果。

【范文2】

My Home

（1）My dad and mom live on the ground floor. The top floor is our guest house. The saying 'East or West, home is the best' is true in more ways than one. Home offers affection and security. My home to me is the best place in the world, where I live with my mother, father, a brother and a sister. I belong to a middle class family. My home is a cozy little flat on the 1st floor in Lajpat Nagar in Delhi.

（2）Our drawing-cum-dining room is tastefully decorated. It has a TV set, a sofa, a refrigerator and a dining table. The decoration pieces remind me of our visits to various places. There are two bedrooms. One is used by my parents and the other is shared by the three of us. The study-table is used by my brother and sister as well for their homework. The kitchen is small but the big windows let in air and sunshine. The wall cupboards help in keeping it tidy. Ours is a small and happy family, where every member is considerate of the needs and comforts of others. We all share household work too. Our mornings are busy and everybody rushes about doing one's work and takes hurried breakfasts when ready. But we all have our dinner together. We share all that we enjoyed or suffered during the day. We keep our home clean and tidy. Everything is kept in place.

（3）This is my home.（Source: https://studymoose.com/my-home-essay）

【点评】

本文是"三段式"文体的习作。全文都是在介绍、说明我的家，是一篇不错的说明文。

本文的主题思想句子是"My home is a cozy little flat on the 1st floor in Lajpat Nagar in Delhi.（我家住在新德里Lajpat Nagar一个温馨的公寓里，我家在一楼）"。正文部分比较详细地描述了我的家为什么cozy（温馨）。作者用了不多的笔墨，详细地介绍了家的布局，各房间的分布和功能，同时还介绍了作者本人及家人在家里都做什么。结尾句没有感叹I love my home, 那样的话就成了议论文。

【范文3】

Life at Home

（1）I live in a small village. Our house is a small building of two stories with white mosaic walls and a red roof. **Let me share some of my life routines at home.**

（2）**Life in the village is simple but interesting.** In front of our house, there are some tall coconut trees with some coconuts on them. I can often hear birds singing in the trees. I often play under the tree and do the reading on the stone stool in the morning. There is a plot of field to the right which is grown with some cabbages. Sometimes I help my parents work in the fields. To the left of my home, it's a piece of land with lichi trees. Every summer when the lichi's are ripe, I go and collect them. They taste so nice. There is a stream behind my house which flows gently. The water is clean and we can see some fish swimming in it. I like to play in the clean water with my friends.

（3）**A country lane extends from my house to the village entrance and you may find it at the end of the lane.**

【点评】

本文使用的是"三段式"写作格式，在习作阶段是可以接受的一篇不错的范例。第一段介绍背景，引起读者的阅读兴趣，主题思想句"Let me share some of my life routines at home."总起全文。

由于本文是说明文，作者没有用太多的形容词、副词来赞美自己的家乡；其立场是中立的和客观的，好似一个导游只讲解不评论，我的家乡好不好读者自己看。

第二大段是正文。正文由 "Life in the village is simple and interesting." 作为引领句，作者适可而止，没有渲染，再多一点描写就成了描写文了。这部分作者主要描写了家乡的生活经历，描绘了几个生活场景，是一篇描写性的说明文。

最后一段，作者没有忘记给读者指路，但没有写 "Welcome to my village! Welcome to my home for a stay." 那样写就成了议论文了。

【范文4】

My Dog, Romeo

My dog, Romeo, is the best pet anyone could have. He is beautiful and easy to care for. Playing with him is lots of fun. He always takes care of me. **There isn't a better pet anywhere.**

Romeo is a beautiful tricolor Sheltie. He is mostly black with white and a bit of brown. Caring for him is easy because I simply have to make sure he has fresh water and food every day. I exercise him by throwing his toys. Romeo is a good pet because he is nice looking and doesn't require much care.

Romeo is lots of fun to play with. He loves to play catch. He follows me around the house with a toy and drops it on my foot so I will kick it. He can catch just about anything, but his favorite is chasing a Frisbee. I really have fun playing with Romeo.

Romeo takes care of me. He always follows me when I leave a room. When I am sitting on the couch he plops down right beside me. When we are outside in the woods he always makes sure that I keep up with the rest of the family. He always watches out for me.

As you can see, Romeo is a great pet. I am proud of him and he doesn't require much care. Playing with him is always enjoyable. He watches over me and keeps me safe. **Romeo is absolutely the best pet anyone could even have!**

【点评】

本文是典型的"五段式"说明文。作者用还算不错的文笔为我们展现了一个可爱好动又会关心主人的宠物狗狗。由于本文中有一些抒情的成分，所以应该说没有严格按照说明文的要求来写。但是描写文和说明文本来就比较难以界定，对于一篇习作来说已经很不错了，可以接受。

本文共有五段，中心思想句是 "There isn't a better pet anywhere.（我的狗狗是世界上最好的狗狗）"。正文部分有三段从小狗狗的可爱的外形、好玩伴和会黏人三个不同的侧面支撑了主题，详细地介绍了我的小狗狗为什么是最棒的。其中每段第一句是本段的主题句，后面举例说明主题句。每段的主题句是全文中心思想句的支撑句。本文段落之间连接较好，安排逻辑性强，层次分明，条理清楚。通过三个段落（即三个侧面）把中心思想解释得清清楚楚、明明白白，让读者看过本文以后也想把Romeo带回家。

阅读与写作训练

一、拓展阅读

Please find the thesis statement of the following expository essay and topic sentence of the supporting paragraphs.（试析下列说明文的中心思想句以及各支撑段的主题句。）

1. My Wishes

Everybody has their own wishes.

I have three wishes which are very close to my heart. Every day I pray to god that my wishes one day will come true. I also try to focus and work hard to achieve my wishes. My father used to tell me that it is also very important to keep working on my dreams so that one day you achieve it.

My first wish is to become the class monitor. Every month our teacher selects one boy or girl as the class monitor. I am a bit naughty in class and my teacher promised me that if I am obedient in the class for the next two weeks she will pick me as class monitor. So I am trying control myself and achieve my first dream.

My second wish is to become a football player and play for the country. Ever since I watched the world cup football matches, I want to become a football player. I used to play football with my friends in my backyard and also in school.

I already talked to my mother about my wish and she permitted me to join a coaching camp nearby. She also made me promise that I will not lose my focus in studies.

My third wish is to visit my dream Disneyland. Every time I see Disneyland in television, I wish I was there. I really hope that one day my parents will take me to my dream land.

These are my three wishes in life. (Source: https://studymoose.com/my-home-essay)

2. My House

There are many kinds of houses which differ in their looks, features and lots of other things. But no matter how much they look different, they all have the same definition, the place where you feel safe, comfortable and settled. As for me, I like modern houses. They are, in my opinion, more up-to-date and more attractive. I live in a spacious modern two-stories house in the center of Saudi Arabia's capital city, Riyadh.

When people look at my house from the street, they see, right away, the high trees around my house and the brickwork roof of it. When you enter the front door you can see the huge chandelier in the top of the entrance hallway. Also, you'll definitely notice the white marbled stairs up to the first floor. In the first floor, there are two bedrooms, one bathroom and a large living room. The living room, which is the room that I really like in my house, has two big sofas and a very nice massage chair. And with an amazingly huge LCD screen in it, it is quite nice for watching movies and having some popcorn at night!

My home, for me, is very important. Everyday when I come back from work and close my front door, I have a nice feeling that my day was special. Without a house that you like, you can never go on with your life. Home is the place where we are born and live. It is the sweetest place in the world. When we sense danger elsewhere we find safety in our home. When there is joy, we share it with other members of our home.

Everybody loves home. For this reason are English poet has written: "Home,

home, sweet home, There is no place like home. " (Source: https://studymoose.com)

3. My Pet Cat

My pet cat, Jersy is a Maine Coon Cat. It is dark brown and black in color. She is quite active and playful. She spends most of her time with me and is, therefore, more affectionate towards me than any of my other family members.

Why we brought Home a Pet Cat? Many of my friends and neighbors had pets at their home and I also longed to have one. I often told my mother to get home a pup or a kitten and she always dismissed my wish saying she doesn't have time to look after it.

When my brother went to the hostel for higher studies, I felt quite lonely. My father went to the office and my mother was engrossed in the household tasks most of the time. I did not have anyone to play and felt the need of having a pet all the more. I again requested my parents to get me a pet. Looking at how lonely I had grown ever since my brother had gone to the hostel, they decided to fulfill my wish. I was overjoyed at hearing this. It is then that Jersy came into our lives. It has been with us for over four years now.

My Pet Cat is Playful Yet Disciplined. Jersy is extremely fond of playing while at the same time it is also quite well-behaved. Many cats run around the house breaking things. However, Jersy makes sure she does not cause any such damage. She also takes instructions. My mother serves her lunch at sharp every day. Jersy goes and sits near her feeder around the same time every day. She finishes her food and makes sure it does not spill around.

Jersy has won the heart of all my family members. She awaits my return from school every afternoon and is delighted to see me back. I am also eager to meet her. We love and enjoy each other's company. (Source: https://www.indiacelebrating.com)

4. My Home

My home is situated in the middle of the village.

There are six members in our family. They are my father, mother, grand-father, grand-mother, my sister and myself. I am the second and the youngest child of my parents. So, being the youngest member, I enjoy love and affection of all. My father is an advocate. My mother is a teacher. She works in the Primary School in our village. My sister is a student. She reads in Women's College. My grand-mother and grand-father love my parents. I am their favourite grand son. We live in a thatched house. The house indicates the simplicity of our family. It has mud walls.

There are four rooms excluding the drawing room and the kitchen. My parents share the room adjoining the kitchen. My grand-mother and grand-father share the room near the drawing room. Another room is used as the store room. There is a spacious courtyard. We have also a cowshed with two cows and a little calf. I respect my parents and old grand-parents. I always obey their commands. My mother and grand-mother do not like to part with me for a moment. When I go to school, my grand-mother accompanies me up to the school. She waits for me at the school gate during the last period. My mother cooks food for us.

As she is a teacher, she prepares food in the morning and preserves it properly for lunch. My sister who stays in the college hostel often comes and helps my mother in her work. I sometimes play interesting jokes with my grand-father and grand-mother. I am very fond of our garden. I water the flower plants at my leisure. When my grand-father goes to the cowshed, I go with him. I often kiss the little calf. When someone of my home falls ill, I take proper care. My uncle comes to our family every month. He brings sweets for me. Sometimes the friends of my father come and take dinner here.

My father is a good host. On my birthday my mother invites other teachers of her school. They all come and share the joy with us. All the villagers respect my home. They say that ours is an ideal home. (Source: https://www.indiacelebrating.com)

5. Sample Obituary

Elaine Brown, 57, died 15th February 2007 at her home in Leyland, near Preston, Lancashire after a short illness. Her funeral service will be held this Friday at St Georges Church, New Road, Chorley, Preston followed by internment at Hill Road Cemetery, Preston

Mrs. Brown was born on 12th July, 1950 in Glasgow, Scotland to Mary and Graham Smith. She gained a first class law degree from Manchester University in 1970 and had a successful career as a practice lawyer specialising in family law. She married David Brown on December 8th 1972. They raised 3 daughters and went on to foster more than 25 children. Mrs Brown moved to Leyland in 1980 and was heavily involved in the local community working with disadvantaged children and was also a member of the local Rotary. In her spare time she enjoyed watercolour painting.

Her family paid this tribute to her, "Elaine was one of the kindest people you could ever meet, she opened her heart and her home to many children over the years and she will be sorely missed."

She is survived by her husband and 3 daughters, Marie, Kim and Samantha.

二、结构练习

Find the thesis statement of the expository essay and provide a brief comment on how the body paragraphs support the thesis.（找出下列议论文的中心思想句并试析各支撑段是怎样支撑中心思想句的。）

1. Mother

A mother is the first, foremost and best friend in everyone's life as no one can be true and real like her. She is the one and the only person who always stands with us in all our good and bad times. She always cares and loves us more than anyone in her life. She always gives us first priority in her life and gives us a glimpse of hope in our bad times. The day we are born, it is our mother who becomes happy more than anyone else. She knows all our reasons for happiness and sadness and tries to make us happy every time.

Mother is the bond of love between Mother and children. There is a special bond that exists between a mother and her child which can never be ended. A mother could never decrease her love and care towards her children and always gives an equal amount of love and care to every kid of her but we all kids together can never give her a little love and care like her in her old age. Even then she never understands us wrong and forgives us like a small child. She understands each and every activity of ours and we can never fool her easily.

A mother never wants us to get hurt by anyone and teaches us to behave well with others. In order to pay attention and pay thankfulness to the mothers, May 13th has been declared as Mother's Day which is celebrated every year. No one pays even a single role in our life as a mother. We too must always take care of our mother all through life. (Source: https://www.indiacelebrating.com)

2. A Career to Make Life Worth Living

Many teenagers spend a lot of time contemplating what they want to do when they graduate from high school. I am fortunate in that I already know; I decided to become a veterinarian when I was two or three years old. Just like humans, animals need people to treat them with the respect and dignity they deserve, and I want to be one of those people. Because of this, I am doing all I can at Reavis to lay the groundwork for my success in college. Then, once I am in college, I will study and learn about all species of animals. Finally, I will find happiness in my career as a veterinarian because when animals need my assistance, I know that I will be able to help them.

First, as a freshman at Reavis High School, I keep in mind my lifelong dream of becoming a veterinarian. I have been taking my education here very seriously, because I know that a person needs to be not only knowledgeable, but also extremely disciplined in order to become a veterinarian. Because of this, I work hard to earn good grades, I take pride in my work, and I have learned to manage my time properly. These skills will be particularly valuable when I enter college.

After leaving Reavis, I must attend college because it is definitely a requirement for becoming a veterinarian. In fact, a bachelor's degree is necessary in order to even enter a veterinarian program. One must also possess excellent communication, leadership, public speaking, and organizational skills. I have put a lot of thought and consideration into college, and I have decided that I would like to go to the University of Illinois. It is a wonderful school, and they even have a graduate program designed for students who want to become veterinarians.

Once I have completed a veterinarian program, I will be able to pursue my dream career. This career provides numerous benefits, the first of which is salary. The average veterinarian salary is $60,000 a year, a salary that would definitely allow me to live a comfortable life. Secondly, it is a rewarding job. This job would provide me with the satisfaction of knowing that I am helping or saving an animal's life. Finally, becoming a veterinarian would assure me a lifetime of happiness. I know I would love going to my job every day, because I would be working with what I love most: animals.

In summary, when I graduate from Reavis, I plan to go to college to become a veterinarian. I love animals and I want to do anything that I can to help them. I know I am only a freshman, but I also know that I am growing up quickly. As Ferris Bueller quotes, "Life moves pretty fast. If you don't stop and look around once in a while, you could miss it!"

3. How Can I Learn to Write an Expository Essay

In the media center-in the media center there will be two places where you can look for example expository papers. First of all, ask the media specialist if they have archived compositions. If they do, make some copies of the ones that fit your needs. If they do not, then you can move to the reference section of the library. There will be books, which have example compilations of different types of writings. Sit down and review these models.

From a peer—if you have a peer who is good at writing, then you have instant and nearby help. Ask your peer if you may use one of his or her old pieces for a model. You can use it and later on return the favor for your friend. Make sure your friend knows that you are not going to copy the paper, just use it as a model for guidance.

Online—you can find every sample of writing in existence online. There are thousands out there. You want to proceed online with caution. You will need to know that the example is properly written and that the person who wrote it was qualified to write it. Modeling after a bad paper is a bad move, which will equal a very bad grade.

From the textbook—textbooks, online and in print, all have supplemental materials in the back of the textbook. All you have to do is turn to the back of your writing or your grammar book and you will find what you need.

A writing company—you can hire a writing company to give you examples of the high school papers that you need. This little-known fact can result in a professional style expository essay. The price will not be too high and you can rest easy knowing that a professional wrote the essay. Partial examples will be on the business website if you do not want to buy a sample one.

4. Global Warming

Ⅰ. Introduction

Global warming is when carbon dioxide, greenhouse gases, and other pollutants in the atmosphere consume the sunlight that is recoiled of the earth's surface. Generally, the radiation would bounce back to space, but these gases that last for centuries in the atmosphere, suck the heat which makes the temperature warm.

Over the past few centuries, humans have changed the earth's temperature in dramatic ways resulting in global warming. There should be a balance between the radiation that the earth receives from the space and the radiation that bounces back to space. 30% of the radiation is immediately reflected back to space by clouds, ice, snow, and other reflective surfaces. The remaining 70% of the radiation is absorbed by the land, oceans, and atmosphere. As the Earth heats up, it releases heat in the form of thermal radiation which passes out of the atmosphere into space. Without atmospheric equilibrium, Earth would be as cold as Moon or as hot as Venus.

Ⅱ. Greenhouse Effect on Global Warming

Greenhouse receives heat in the form of UV radiation of the sun. The UV rays pass easily from the transparent glasses of the greenhouse and get absorbed by the plants. Weaker radiation gets trapped inside the glasses thus warming the greenhouse. The greenhouse effect is the natural process that warms the temperature of the earth. The natural greenhouse gases in the atmosphere cause 33°C elsius warmer temperature than it would be in its absence.

Ⅲ. Enhanced Green House Effect

Our current problem is the enhanced greenhouse effect due to human activities like burning fossil fuels, overuse of natural resources, clearing forests, farming, etc. that are increasing the concentrations of greenhouse gases. Greenhouse gases include carbon dioxide, nitrous oxide, ozone, methane, water vapor and chemicals such as CFCs.

Ⅳ. Conclusion

It is a fact that burning fossil fuels like oil, coal, and gas release greenhouse gases in the atmosphere. The gases raise the temperature of the atmosphere. The switch to renewable resources for energy such as wind energy, solar energy, and hydropower will help to moderate the demand for fossil fuels which will cut down the emission of greenhouse gases. We can also contribute by planting trees, saving electricity, using public transport instead of a car, and creating awareness to prevent global warming. (Source: https://www.indiacelebrating.com)

Divide the following essay into suitable paragraphs.（阅读下列文章，并把它分成适当的段落。）

Charcoal is produced by burning wood slowly in a low-oxygen environment. This material, which is mainly carbon, was used for many years to heat iron ore to extract the metal. But when Abraham Darby discovered a smelting process using coke (produced from coal) in 1709 demand for charcoal collapsed. At approximately the same time the carbon dioxide level in the atmosphere began to rise. But a new use for charcoal, re-named biochar, has recently emerged. It is claimed that using biochar made from various types of plants can both improve soil quality and combat global warming. Various experiments in the United States have shown that adding burnt crop wastes to soil increases fertility and cuts the loss of vital nutrients such as nitrates. The other benefit of biochar is its ability to lock CO_2 into the soil. The process of decay normally allows the carbon dioxide in plants to return to the atmosphere rapidly, but when transformed into charcoal this may be delayed for hundreds of years. In addition, soil containing biochar appears to release less methane, a gas which contributes significantly to global warming.

American researchers claim that widespread use of biochar could reduce global CO_2 emissions by over 10 per cent. But other agricultural scientists are concerned about the environmental effects of growing crops especially for burning, and about the displacement of food crops that might be caused. However, the potential twin benefits of greater farm yields and reduced greenhouse gases mean that further research in this area is urgently needed.

三、写作练习

Ⅰ. **Guided Writing.**（手把手教写作。）

1. My new mobile phone is of _____. It _____ .

I can _____ but I can't _____ .

2. To make Chinese food you need to do:

（1）Go to the market and _____ ；

（2）Wash _____ ；

（3）Light the fire and _____ ：

（4）Put _____ ；

Now, you get a nice dish of Chinese food.

3. The saying "East or West, home is the best" is true in more ways than one. Home offers affection and security. My home to me is _____ .

_____

_____ .

Our house _____ . The decoration _____ .

We _____ at home. We can also _____ and _____ together.

It is the sweetest place in the world. When we sense danger elsewhere we find safety in our home. When there is joy, we share it with other members of our home. Everybody loves their home.

4. A hobby is _____. It is _____ .

My hobby is _____

I liked _____ when I was a little child and I _____ .Today,

_____ and it helps a lot _____ .

Ⅱ. **Write a expository essay using prompts given below.**（用所给写作范围要求写一篇说明文。）

1. Everybody has got dreams. Dream is the motivation for progress in people's life. Write an expository essay about your dreams.

2. You are going to buy a new car, please introduce the car to your readers.

3. You saw a good movie online recently, please share it with your readers.

4. Please write an expository essay on one book you read with your audience.

四、判断题

Identify which type of writing is being described.（根据下面的描述说一说是什么文体。）

1. _____ A story about the time you got lost at Disneyland

2. _____ A web page telling how to create a web page

3. _____ The Harry Potter books

4. _____ A letter to the governor explaining why the tax increase is a bad idea

5. _____ Writing in which you record details of a trip taken

6. _____ An essay discussing a theme from Romeo and Juliet

7. _____ An article attempting to convince readers to boycott a store chain

8. _____ A poem about the sights and sounds of rainfall

9. _____ A paper about the horrible treatment of the people in Guantanamo

10. _____ The cover story in the morning newspaper

11. _____ A brochure advertising a luxury hotel and resort

12. _____ A paper discussing the after effects of a war

五、阅读与理解

Read and judge what style the paragraphs or essays are and say in what way the expository essays are different from descriptive ones.（阅读下列段落或文章，说一说它们是什么文体以及说明文与描写文有什么区别。）

1. Peacock

The peacock can be found everywhere. They have colourful feathers, two legs and a small beak. They are famous for their dance. When a peacock dances it spreads its feathers like a fan. It has a long shiny dark blue neck. Peacocks are mostly found in the fields they are very beautiful birds. The females are known as a peahen. Their feathers are used for making jackets, purses etc. We can see them in a zoo.

2. Ants

Ants are found everywhere in the world. They make their home in buildings, gardens etc. They live in anthills. Ants are very hardworking insects. Throughout the summers they collect food for the winter season. Whenever they find a sweet lying on the floor they stick to the sweet and carry it to their home. Thus, in this way, they clean the floor. Ants are generally red and black in colour. They have two eyes and six legs. They are social insects. They live in groups or colonies. Most ants are scavengers they collect whatever food they can find. They are usually wingless but they develop wings when they reproduce. Their bites are quite painful.

3. Camels

The camels are called the "ships of the desert". They are used to carry people and loads from one place to another. They have a huge hump on their body where they! Store their fat. They can live without water for many days. Their thick fur helps them to stop the sunshine from warming their bodies. Camels have long necks and long legs. They have two toes on each foot. They move very quickly on sand. They eat plants, grasses and bushes. They do not' harm anyone. Some of the camels have two humps. These camels are called! Bactrian camels.

4. Elephant

An elephant is the biggest living animal on land. It is quite huge in size. It is usually black or grey in colour. Elephants have four legs, a long trunk and two white tusks near their trunk. Apart from this, they have two big ears and a short tail. Elephants are vegetarian. They eat all kinds of plants especially bananas. They are quite social, intelligent and useful animals. They are used to carry logs of wood from one place to another.

They are good swimmers.

5. Horses

Horses are farm animals. They are usually black, grey, white and brown in colour. They are known as beasts of burden. They carry people and goods from one place to another. They have long legs, which are very strong. They can easily run long distances. Horses have hard hoofs which protect their feet. They like eating grass and grams they are used in sports like polo and hors riding. An adult male horse is called a stallion and an adult female is called a mare whereas the female baby horse is called a foal and a male baby horse is called a colt. Horses usually move in herds. They live in a stable. They are very useful animals.

6. Dogs

The Dog is a pet animal. It is one of the most obedient animals. There are many kinds of dogs in the world. Some of them are very friendly while some of them a dangerous. Dogs are of different color like black, red, white and brown. Some old them have slippery shiny skin and some have rough skin. Dogs are carnivorous animals. They like eating meat. They have four legs, two ears and a tail. Dogs are trained to perform different tasks. They protect us by guarding our house. They are loving animals. A dog is called man's best friend. They are used by the police to find hidden things. They are one of the most useful animals in the world.

7. Stars

The stars are tiny points of light in the space. On a clear night we can see around 2,000 to 3,000 stars without using a telescope. Stars look tiny in the sky because they are far away from the Earth. In ancient times the sky watchers found patterns of stars in the sky. These astronauts Neil Armstrong and patterns of people and the creatures from the myths and the legends. As the Earth spins from east to west the stars also appear to cross from east to west. The stars are made up of gases.

练习答案

第一编

第一章　第一节

练习一

1. Smoking is harmful to your health.

2. These few examples show that school does not always predict failure in life.

3. In the past few years, social networking sites such as MySpace, Facebook, and Twitter have become hugely popular across all ages.

4. Drama languished in Europe after the fall of Rome during the fifth and sixth centuries.

5. One form of distraction is imagery.

6. Surtsey was born in 1963.

7. We can make mistakes at any age.

8. Knowing about yourself means not only that you find what you are good at and what you like, it also means discovering what you are not good at and what you don't like.

练习二

1. Everyone lives by selling something.

2. Different countries and different races have different manners.

第一章　第二节

练习一（略）

练习二（略）

练习三（略）

第二章　第一节

练习一

4-2-3-1-5

练习二　1

1. Initially

2. Later

3. In the eighteenth century

4. But recently

练习二　2

1. First　　2. But

3. also　　4. For example

5. And finally

练习二　3

1. early　　　　2. First

3. This calculation　4. Then

5. Finally

练习三　4

练习四

（1）为主题句。（2）（3）（6）（7）（9）（10）为意连，（5）（8）为形连。

第三章　第一节

练习一

1. Cheating in exams hurts yourself and discourages others.

2. So, we should not buy takeout food.

练习二（略）

练习三（略）

第六章　第一节

1. Trees lay on the side of the road and they looked as if they had been pulled out of the ground by huge machines.

Trees lay on the side of the road. They looked as if they had been pulled out of the ground by huge machines.

2. Every wall was smashed to rubble and the only thing left of those houses was the land and the rocks from the rubble.

Every wall was smashed to rubble. The only thing left of those houses was the land and the rocks from the rubble.

3. The town looked deserted and the streets were so dark and empty that the only thing we could hear was the wind blowing.

The town looked deserted. The streets were so dark and empty that the only thing we could hear was the wind blowing.

4. We worked from dusk to dawn and never had so many contracts been written in such a short time.

5. Money continued to flow in and we started to live the life of the rich. On weekends we ate at expensive restaurants.

6. The river extended beyond the mountains and we saw the clouds merge with the water in the horizon.

The river extended beyond the mountains. We saw the clouds merge with the water in the horizon.

7. Caffeine supplies the principal stimulant and it increases the capacity for muscular and mental work without harmful reaction.

191

Caffeine supplies the principal stimulant, it increases the capacity for muscular and mental work without harmful reaction.

8. Like all good things in life, the drinking of coffee may be abused. Those having an idiosyncratic susceptibility to alkaloids should be temperate in the use of tea, coffee, or cocoa.

9. Some people cannot eat strawberries and that would not be a valid reason for a general condemnation of strawberries.

Some people cannot eat strawberries. That would not be a valid reason for a general condemnation of strawberries.

第六章　第二节

练习一

1. A　2. A　3. A　4. A　5. A
6. B　7. A　8. B　9. B　10. B
11. A　12. A　13. A　14. A and B
15. A　16. A　17. A　18. A
19. A　20. B

练习二

1. F　2. T　3. F　4. T　5. T

练习三

1. Most tarantulas live in the tropics, but several species occur in the temperate zone and a few are common in the southern United States.

2. Typically, shopping centers are designed with one or more large department stores as magnets. These are located among the smaller stores to encourage impulse buying.

3. Both divorced mothers and divorced fathers have legitimate concerns, but their radically different viewpoints create poor communication between angry spouses.

4. All societies—whether primitive, agricultural, or industrial—use energy. They make things, and they distribute things.

5. Congress passed the bill after long hours of debate, and there were strong convictions on both sides.

6. The railroads, highways, and cities that will spring up may divert attention. However, they cannot cover up society's decay.

7. I looked across the fire lane at a section that had been burned three weeks before, and the ground was already covered with light green.

8. Homelessness itself is often the precipitating factor. For example, many pregnant women without

homes are denied care because they constantly travel from one shelter to another.

第六章 第三节

练习一

1. A 2. B 3. B 4. A 5. A
6. A 7. A 8. A 9. A 10. A

练习二

1. Looking up to the sky, they saw some clouds floating up above their heads.

2. After I cleaned the room, my dog wanted to take a walk.

3. While it was flying in the sky, I shot the bird.

4. When I was seven, my mother gave birth to my brother.

5. While I was having an English class, Jim phoned me.

6. While I was driving, my tire went flat.

7. When we were swimming in the river, the boat floats away.

8. While I was sleeping, the pet dog ran loose and never came back.

第六章 第五节

练习一

1. My uncle Julius likes bagels, lox, and salad.

2. Every day，Bill runs five miles, consumes eight thousand calories.

3. Jose's daughter will either attend Harvard or attend Standford.

4. Fatima's knowledge of accounting is greater than Farah's.

5. Stephen King's book reviews were as positive as Asimov's.

6. The house sitter lost the keys, neglected the dogs, and trashed the kitchen.

7. Andrew was an industrious student, an excellent athlete.

8. She was a beautiful, spoiled child.

9. A math book with practice problems and a good index is useful.

10. Customers may climb the stairs, ride the escalator, or take the elevator.

11. Jake knew he had to run or stay to face the consequences.

12. To sleep and eat were his main occupations.

13. Either he should do it or I will do it.

14. Her ambition was to act in movies and to write a book about her experiences.

15. Mary likes to paint, sew, and play the piano.

16. That mask will scare Billy, scare the cat.

练习二

1. F, T   2. F, T   3. T, F

4. T, F   5. F, T   6. T, F

第二编

第一章   第一节

练习一（略）

练习二（略）

练习三   第一题（略）

练习三   第一题   1

1. hunter

2. both brave and hard-working

3. forest

4. catch

5. run away

6. steep cliff

7. transformed

8. became husband and wife

9. Ever since then

练习三   第一题   2

1. there lived a monster

2. both ugly and greedy

3. do nothing about that

4. on their way

5. heard of the story

6. that he decided to catch

7. came again and asked for nice food and beautiful women

8. beaten and caught

9. lived happily

练习三   第二题（略）

练习四（略）

第二章

练习一（略）

练习二（略）

练习三

第一题（略）

第二题

1. In fact

2. Moreover

3. In other words

4. However

5. Furthermore

6. In addition

7. As time goes by

8. Fore example

9. Consequently

10. Fortunately

11. To sum up

12. Moreover

第三题（略）

练习四（略）

第三章

练习一（略）

练习二（略）

练习三（略）

第四章

练习一（略）

练习二（略）

练习三（略）

练习四

1. narrative

2. expository

3. narrative

4. argumentative

5. descriptive

6. argumentative

7. persuasive

8. descriptive

9. expository

10. narrative

11. expository

12. argumentative

参考文献

[1]CaMLASamples Essays and Commentary[EB/OL]. www. CambridgeMichidge.org.

[2]Stephen Bailey. Academic Writing(Third edition)[M]. London and New York: Routledge Taylor & Francis Group, 2011.

[3]Lauren Starkey. How To Write Great Essays[M].New York: Learning Express, LLC., 2004.

[4]Edward D. Johnson. The Handbook of Good English[M]. New York: Facts On File, Inc., 1991.

[5]Desmond A. Gilling. Essential Handbook For Business Writing[M]. Canada: Greenlink Consulting, 2013.

[6]Patricia Wilcox Peterson.Developing Writing [M].Washington, DC: Office of English Language Programs, 2003.

[7]Marion Field.Improve your Written English[M].Oxford: How To Content, 2009.

[8]Steve Barrett, Shari Barrett. Put That in Writing [M]. New York: Barrett's Bookshelf, 2009.

[9]Don E. WilsonBat [EB/OL]. (Feb. 12, 2020). https://www.britannica.com/ animal/bat-mammal#accordion-article-history.

[10]EditorBat/[EB/OL]. https://symbolism.fandom.com/wiki/Bat.

[11]Factmonster EditorBats [EB/OL].（Feb. 21, 2017）.https://www. factmonster.com/bats.

[12]Editor BATS - MYTHS, FOLKLORE AND FACTS [EB/OL]. http:// www.crystalwind.ca/ mystical-magical/legends-fables-and-lore/folklore/bats-myths-folklore-and-facts.